10-10-83

.7 + .7 (1.7) × .7 + .7(1.7) × .9 + .9(-.9)

.91 x.91 x.99

THE POLITICAL ECONOMY OF REAGANOMICS

THE POLITICAL ECONOMY OF REAGANOMICS

A CRITIQUE

Stephen Rousseas

M. E. Sharpe INC. ARMONK, NEW YORK
LONDON

Copyright © 1982 by M. E. Sharpe, Inc.
80 Business Park Drive, Armonk, New York 10504

All rights reserved. No part of this book may be reproduced in any form without written permission from the publisher.

Library of Congress Cataloging in Publication Data

Rousseas, Stephen William.
    The political economy of Reagonomics.

    1. Supply-side economics. I. Title.
HB241.R68 1982   338.973   82-10659
ISBN: 0-87332-227-4
ISBN: 0-87332-239-8 (pbk.)

Printed in the United States of America

to
ANARGE
who
would have
agreed

Contents

Preface	ix
Chapter 1: . . . . . The Crisis of Faith	3
Chapter 2: . . . . . Classical Supply-Side Economics	22
Chapter 3: . . . . . Demand-Side Economics	47
Chapter 4: . . . . . Monetarist Supply-Side Economics	66
Chapter 5: . . . . . Supply-Side Praxis	88
Chapter 6: . . . . . The Great Confession and Its Aftermath	101
Chapter 7: . . . . . The Threat of Delegitimation	118
About the Author	145

Preface

By the time of its first anniversary, the Reagan administration was embattled. The idea that the budget would be balanced by 1984 had been abandoned. The President, contrary to his own convictions and campaign promise, now calls deficits "a necessary evil." Like all presidents before him, he has been forced by circumstances to give up on the idea of a balanced budget. If that were all there was to it, there would be no need to write a book about it.

What is different this time is that the present administration is engaged in a major counterrevolution. It is seeking to undo the last half-century of social progress on the ground that the big government it entailed has itself become the cause of all our ills—inflation, unemployment, a public debt that is forever rising, high interest rates, and low growth. In seeking solutions to these problems, the President embraced a new school of thought—*supply-side economics*. It is the purpose of this book to examine critically the ideology behind this "new" economics.

As will be argued in *The Political Economy of Reaganomics*, supply-side economics is not a coherent system of thought—nor is it "new." The two main branches are what I call the classical and the monetarist supply-side schools. They are not in agreement. Indeed, there are fundamental differences between them, which have now surfaced into an ugly struggle for the President's attention. In addition to these two schools, there are the orthodox, Old Guard budget-balancers who disagree with the supply-siders on the importance of the deficit and the wisdom of the supply-side tax cut that was steamrollered through Congress in 1981. Budget-balancers are to be found in both houses of Congress, in the Federal Reserve under Paul Volcker, in the Office of Management and Budget under David Stockman, and in an informal group of presidential councillors consisting of former high officials of the Eisenhower, Nixon, and Ford administrations.

What has emerged is a three-way struggle that has yet to be resolved. I have tried to provide the reader with the theoretical background against which the drama is being played out. A sophisticated command of economic theory is not required. The book is designed for the generally informed reader, and technical matters, when they could not be avoided, have been kept as simple as possible. Chapter 3, which can be skipped, gives a summary view of the main "demand-side" theories which supply-side economics is supposed to have supplanted. Though it is not absolutely necessary in order to understand the other chapters of the book, a quick reading might prove helpful.

The book is, essentially, a study in political economy, in the sense that economics cannot be separated from politics. I do not regard economics as an independent science; it is permeated at all levels with ideology, the "scientific" pretentiousness of economic theory notwithstanding.

As a Post Keynesian, I have been very critical of supply-side economics and I have tried to be systematic in my criticisms. Whether they will convince the reader is another matter, but convincing or not I think they are important for understanding the counterrevolution that has been launched under the banner of Ronald Reagan and the perils it poses for the country.

* * * *

I would like to acknowledge the permission of the *Journal of Post Keynesian Economics* and *Challenge* magazine to incorporate two of my earlier articles on supply-side economics. I am also grateful to the University of the South for sponsoring a conference I was asked to participate in last October. In particular I am indebted to Alfred Eichner of Rutgers University for having prodded me to do the book and then having given generously of his time in reading the manuscript, and to my colleagues at Vassar College, Marc Jarsulic and David Merriell, the latter having read the manuscript as a noneconomist. Above all, I want to thank Sidney Weintraub of the University of Pennsylvania for having gotten me started on the subject last summer and for his many kindnesses to me.

I would also like to thank a former student of mine at Vassar College, Miss Anne Rendall, who was instrumental in providing me with an enormous amount of valuable material from the Treasury Department. Finally, my thanks to Mrs.Judy Thorson, who uncomplainingly typed several versions of the manuscript under difficult conditions.

Stephen Rousseas
Poughkeepsie, N.Y.
May 1982

THE POLITICAL ECONOMY OF REAGANOMICS

> *Our revenue laws have operated in many ways to the unfair advantage of the few, and they have done little to prevent an unjust concentration of wealth and power.*
>
> — Franklin D. Roosevelt

> *The taxing power of the government must not be used to regulate the economy or bring about social change.*
>
> — Ronald Reagan

CHAPTER 1

The Crisis of Faith

I

Prevailing social theories are convenient constructions of reality which seek, more often than not, to justify whatever is by forcing the "facts" of social existence into preconceived ideological boxes. They are, when things are going well, celebrations of the status quo, and the main spokesmen for establishment theory serve as the legitimators of power and those who wield it. Immutable "laws" are propounded which "prove," on scientific grounds, that the system is just, and being just, predestined to go on forever. When things are not going too well, the theoretical guardians of the conventional wisdom tend to scold and to attribute the malfunctioning of the system to violations of sacred maxims.

Such was the state of affairs, a little over fifty years ago, with the onset of the Great Depression. It was by far the greatest challenge American capitalism had to face since the Civil War. On a black Thursday the stock market crash wiped out the paper wealth of the newly rich, and massive bank failures cleaned out the life savings of many of the not-so-rich. Real output fell by one-third, factories closed, and unemployment (as officially measured) soared to 25 percent of the labor force. According to the conventional theory of the time, it could not and should not have happened.

In its purest and most ideal form, capitalism was seen to operate within a system of competitive markets. Markets were simply the institutional arrangements within which buyers and sellers confronted each other. No single participant was big enough, either by the amount of a particular good or service he wished to purchase or the amount he was willing to sell on the market, to have any noticeable effect on price. Power was so widely diffused as not to be a social problem. All prices were determined by the free interplay of individuals in unfettered markets, and all players sought their own individual private gain in total disregard for the welfare of others or, for that matter, for the welfare of society as a whole, which was simply the algebraic sum of the welfare of its constituent parts. The market system automatically assured that the greatest public good was to be derived from the greatest private selfishness. When not tampered with, the market transformed the innate selfishness of man into a natural and unintended harmony of interests.

Such was the theoretical system that Adam Smith had wrought in 1776 when he published his monumental work, the *Wealth of Nations*. The individual, he wrote, "intends only his own security and . . . intends only his own gain, and he is in this . . . led by an invisible hand to promote an end which was not part of his intention." And that unintended "end" was the social welfare, itself the by-product of the free-wheeling forces of an impersonal market system, which also seemed to guarantee an equitable distribution of the social product among all members of society. Above all, as Adam Smith's theoretical system was subsequently refined, capitalism was described as automatically tending toward full employment along a dynamic growth path. Any lapse from this ideal would be automatically corrected by built-in, spontaneous market forces. Changes in relative prices, in other words, would assure the optimal allocation and use of all resources. Short-run changes in the level of real output, and hence employment, by being ephemeral, could therefore be ignored. Capitalism, by its very nature, was in tune with the harmony of the universe. Everything was in exquisite balance. Although the "laws" of economics were patterned after those of Newton, they were different in one essential respect. Unlike the laws of the physical universe, the laws of economics could be violated, with disastrous results.

Adam Smith was not unaware of the great perils confronting freely competitive markets. "People of the same trade," he wrote, "seldom meet together, even for merriment and diversion, but the conversation ends in a conspiracy against the public, or in some contrivance to raise prices." The threat of monopoly was always lurking in the wings. Government, however, was an even greater threat to the market system than the private abuses of monopoly power. In 1876, one hundred years after the publication of the *Wealth of Nations*, the Political Economy Club of London met to honor the event. "One of the great dangers which now hangs over this country," warned the treasurer of the Club, "is that the wholesome spontaneous operation of human interests and human desires seems to be in course of rapid supersession by the erection of one Governmental department over another . . . and by the whole term of Parliament being taken up in attempting to do for the nation those very things which, if the teaching of the man whose name we are celebrating today is to bear any fruit at all, the nation can do much better for itself." It was the role of political economy, as laid out by Adam Smith and his successors, to "reduce the functions of government within a smaller and smaller compass." The chairman of the centennial celebration reinforced the treasurer's inquietudes by stating that the primary and overriding duty of economists lay in "propagating opinions which shall have the effect of confining government within its proper province and preventing it from all manner of aggressions and intrusions upon the province and the free agency of the individual."[1] The sole function of government, it was agreed, was to provide for the national security, to enforce and uphold legal contracts, and to promote civil law and order.

II

These ideas reigned supreme—at least on the level of ideology— up to the crash of 1929. True, panics and cycles were a part of our past, but they were fleeting incidents in a rapidly growing, exuberant economy engaged in the heady process of creative destruction. Cycles were seen as temporary phenomena, an unavoidable part of capitalism to be borne in stoic silence. A leading school of economics attributed them to sunspots. There could thus be no moral public responsibility for the short-run suffering of the mass of people, and, if the poor suffered unduly, it was because of their failure to limit their daily consumption in good times in order to provide for the inevitable rainy days. For others, cycles were purely monetary phenomena attributable to a perverse elasticity of the money supply, which the creation of the Federal Reserve System in 1913 had solved once and for all—or so it was thought. American capitalism, in the 1920s, was seen by the economics profession as marching forward resolutely on a plateau of infinite prosperity. The era of Giant Capitalism in the 1910s was played down; the idealized market system continued to hold sway, at least in the minds of economists. Then came the collapse.

One of the great axioms of our existence is: *What is, is possible, even if a theory says that it is not.* A corollary is: *And if it is possible and does exist, then it is the theory that has to go, not the real world.* Conventional market theory, however, held on. It argued that nothing was wrong with the theory; it was the real world that was out of whack. The "laws" of economics had been transgressed, the economy was living in sin, and the wages of sin are retribution. We were being punished for our evil ways. Apply the antitrust laws, break up the unions, take the government out of the business of running the economy, and market forces would quickly move us back to the natural level of full employment. With flexible market prices, flexible wages, and no governmental interference with market forces, adjustments in relative prices would result in the reallocation of resources needed to restore full employment. The policy recommendations followed logically from the supporting theory, but they were politically naive. No elected government was about to take on big business *and* big labor at the same time. Apart from political considerations, such policies would further wreck the economy by trying to go back to something that had never existed in the first place, except in the mythology of the underlying theory.

The Great Depression could not be denied. It was there in all its black majesty and it was not just another transient rainy day. It was a storm that threatened the very survival of the system and there was no new theory to provide a quick fix; Keynes's *General Theory* (1936) came later. With rejection of the naive policy nostrums of conventional theory, the political response in the United States was a pragmatic groping for solutions which led to that amalgam of policies called the New Deal. Its public works projects, its relief for the poor, its civilian conservation program for unemployed youth, the National Recovery Act (NRA), and the establishment of a social security system—all these gave some measure of hope to a dispirited nation. The federal budget went from a $737 million surplus in 1930 to a $4.5 billion deficit in 1936. The public debt, in the process, more than doubled. It went from $16 billion in 1930 to $34 billion in 1936. By 1940 it had reached $43 billion, a phenomenal amount for its time and one that led to repeated warnings of bankruptcy and impending disaster. Yet, in retrospect, the New Deal did too little rather than too much. After a slow recovery, the U.S. economy dropped sharply once again in 1937. It began its full recovery only in 1939 with the onset of World War II in Europe, and with the direct involvement of the United States in 1941.

As World War II was coming to an end and victory seemed assured, the old fears resurfaced. As a warning to its corporate subscribers, Leo Cherne's Research Institute of America predicted (on expensive linen paper) 11 million people unemployed in the immediate postwar period. The Pabst Blue Ribbon Beer Company announced a competition, with a $25,000 first prize, for the best 2,000-word essay on how to avoid sliding back into the mass unemployment of the prewar period. The National Planning Association was established in Washington and it quickly recruited a staff of professional economists to work on a national plan for the postwar reconversion of the economy. The British White Paper of 1945, for the first time in modern history, proclaimed the government's responsibility to provide for *full* employment in the postwar world, and in the United States the Employment Act of 1946 committed the federal government to the maintenance of *maximum* employment, full employment being too controversial for the U.S. Congress. And in the late 1940s the United Nations convened a Committee of Experts (Nicholas Kaldor, Arthur Smithies, John Maurice Clark, Pierre Uri, and E. Ronald Walker) to propose *National and International Measures for Full Employment*. Governments (particularly the United States) were to be held responsible for the overall high-level performance of their economies, which was to be assured by the adoption of appropriately stabilizing fiscal measures. It was on this basis that we entered the postwar period with some trepidation but armed with the new Keynesian theory for managing aggregate demand. Government was to compensate for the occasional market failings of the capitalist system, with special emphasis on the "free" market's failure to provide for full employment.

Keynesian economics gathered momentum in the postwar period and quickly provided, ex post facto, the intellectual rationale for the earlier pragmatic policies of the New Deal. In a stagnant economy operating at considerably less than full employment, government expenditure and tax policies were to be used to stimulate aggregate demand. Personal income tax cuts would increase disposable income. Consumption expenditures would increase as a result, which, in turn, would stimulate private investment and output. Business tax cuts, on the other hand, would work more directly to spur investment by providing the additional cash flows businessmen needed to finance their capital outlays—thereby moving the economy closer still to full employment. On top of this, government expenditures in the form of public works would provide jobs for the unemployed and pump additional purchasing power into the economy via the construction of dams, roads, city halls, schools, hospitals, and other forms of social capital. Finally, governmental transfer payments in the form of relief for the unemployed would alleviate human suffering in the interim until the economy could get moving again.

The government's impact on output and unemployment would

be primarily through the government budget. Its tool would be an expansionary fiscal policy and deficit financing, and its role would be compensatory—temporarily filling in the gap between actual private outlays and the amount of aggregate demand needed to achieve a full-employment economy. Monetary policy, in this scheme, was to play a lesser role. In the 1930s and the immediate postwar years, the banking system was awash in a sea of liquidity, and it was recognized that additional bank reserves could not of themselves stimulate an increase in the demand for loans without the prior play of fiscal policy.

Prior to the war, the Temporary National Economic Committee (TNEC) in Washington had held hearings on the failure of the economy and published volumes describing interlocking corporate directorships and monopolistic restraints on trade. By the onset of the postwar period, the market system had been discredited and the end of laissez-faire proclaimed. It was no longer believed that there was a natural tendency of capitalism to move toward full employment. Indeed, as viewed within a Keynesian framework, capitalism could well rest at a chronic level of underemployment indefinitely. Theories of secular stagnation abounded, and an increased role of government was seen as the only way out of the morass. This was the state of affairs when World War II broke out. It was left to the postwar period to build on the Keynesian foundation and to refine its policy tools to their highest "fine tuning" degree of "perfection" in the Kennedy administration—until Keynesian theory itself came onto hard times in the 1970s.

III

For the most part, the postwar period was an economic success. The fear of another Great Depression was replaced by a series of mild, short-lived recessions. The trend of real output, real wages, and productivity was upward and inflation, by current standards, was a relatively minor problem. Everyone was a Keynesian, including the Republicans, or so Walter Heller said at the end of his tenure as chairman of Kennedy's Council of Economic Advisors. Then came the 1970s and the problem of stagflation—low growth accompanied by high unemployment and inflation. Keynesian economics itself was now on trial.

A retrospective on the postwar period was held in 1980, on the occasion of the sixtieth anniversary of the influential National Bureau of Economic Research (NBER). At its conference on *The American Economy in Transition*,[2] participants were asked to review the overall postwar performance of the American economy from the point of view of their specialties.

The year 1980 was not a good one. The economy was once again in serious trouble. Echoing the treasurer of the Political Economy Club of London in 1876, Martin Feldstein, a leader of the current counterrevolution and host of the conference as director of the NBER, attributed the poor performance of the American economy to government interference. The worm had turned. "There can be no doubt," he wrote, "that government policies . . . deserve substantial blame for [our] adverse experience" (p. 3). Government regulations, income transfer and social insurance programs, and the inhibiting tax effects on capital accumulation had sapped the vitality of capitalism.

Feldstein's views, however, were hardly reflected in the other papers presented at that conference. Instead of a return to "the years of chaos and depression," the postwar economy, according to Benjamin Friedman, had "entered an era of stability and prosperity" with not only a higher average growth rate in the postwar years "but also a smaller variability of that growth" (pp. 11-13). The "categorical imperative" of postwar policymakers, in the opinion of the late Arthur Okun, was the avoidance of the Great Depression, and in that, he argued, they had largely succeeded. The business cycle had indeed been tamed, or at least brought within politically tolerable limits. This newfound stability, moreover, was greater than at any other time. "The standard deviation of real GNP around its growth trend," wrote Okun, "was about one-fourth as large as it had been in 1900-45, and only half as large as in the 'golden age' of 1900-16, 1920-29." Whereas expansions averaged twenty-six months and contractions twenty-one months from 1854 to 1937, the postwar expansions had an average duration of forty-eight months with contractions compressed to an average of eleven months. "This quantum jump in stability," said Okun, "must . . . be credited to public policy. *It was made in Washington,*" and it was "the compositional shift" to a larger public sector GNP share that constituted "the largest single stabilizing element." The growth of government transfer payments was another factor contributing to the marked reduction in cyclical instability. Although the postwar record of macroeconomic policy "in dealing with relatively minor accidents . . . is mixed," Keynesian monetary and fiscal policy was eminently successful in avoiding catastrophe. To Okun, the success of postwar economic policy was to be measured *"not in dollars of real GNP, but in the survival of United States Capitalism"* (1980, pp. 162-63, 168, italics supplied).

Okun's assessment of the postwar performance of the U.S. economy was reinforced by Alan S. Blinder's analysis of the postwar distribution of income. From 1947 to 1977 "real consumption per capita increased by more than 80 percent." At the same time "the basic necessities of life—food, clothing, and shelter—commanded ever decreasing shares of the consumer budget." The net result was a drastic improvement in "the average level of economic well-being" as well as in its content (p. 433). The increasing levels of per capita real income, however, did not affect the distribution of income which remained virtually unchanged, with a Gini ratio[3] ranging from a low of .40 to a high of .42, with the mean smack in the middle at .41. Although there was little change in the postwar distribution of income, it was "noticeably more equal than the distribution of 1929" (p. 435). Despite this improvement, however, the United States continues to have a higher inequality of income distribution than many other industrialized countries and has the dubious distinction of competing with France for the worst among the Organization for Economic Cooperation and Development (OECD) nations. According to Blinder, "the richest fifth of American families received eight times as much income as the poorest fifth" (p. 436). To Blinder, this constant 8:1 postwar ratio, though better than that in the prewar period, is nevertheless "a very substantial income gap."

The stability of the postwar income distribution is in large part due to government transfer payments—both in kind and in cash, with the latter playing a more significant role. Transfer payments (welfare, aid to dependent children, food stamps, public housing and employment, medical services for the poor, etc.) as a proportion of GNP rose from 0.7 percent in the 1920s to more than 10 percent for 1973 through 1979. To Robert Gordon, "the growth in the size of government after 1947 was mainly reflected in transfer payments rather than in goods and services." The combined spending on goods and services by federal, state, and local governments as a percentage of GNP "exhibited no increase at all between the 1957-67 decade and the most recent 1973-79 subperiod." The increase in the size of government in the postwar economy must therefore be largely attributed to transfer payments—which served the dual function of preventing a deterioration in the distribution of income in the postwar period while simultaneously adding to the stability of demand in the postwar economy. Since "the lower income strata receive a disproportionately large share of transfers," according to Blinder, "it is clear that cash transfers pushed the distribution of income in the direction of greater equality during the postwar period" (p. 446).

But what of the problem of poverty in the postwar era? As Blinder points out, "Income is a continuous variable, whose distribution can be estimated. Poverty, however, is a dichotomous variable: a family is either poor or it is nonpoor. To decide who is poor, we must place a 'poverty line' somewhere in the income distribution . . . and count how many families (or people) fall below it" (p. 454). Whether using the official "absolute" standard of poverty (based on a basket of goods adjusted for inflation) or a "relative" standard of poverty (those with incomes 44 percent below the median income, for example), Blinder finds that, *when transfers are deducted from income*, poverty goes up from 11.8 to 21 percent on the absolute standard and from 15.4 to 24.1 percent on the relative poverty standard. *Government transfer payments must therefore also be seen as a critical factor in the amelioration of poverty.*

In the postwar period, there was a marked decline in officially defined poverty during the 1960s, largely because of the War on Poverty programs of the Johnson administration. Between 1965 and 1976 Blinder found a 24.4 percent decline in the poverty rate, attributed almost in its entirety to increased transfer payments. Without them the poverty rate (expressed as a percentage of all persons living below the official poverty level) would not have declined. In summary, transfer payments are clearly responsible, in great part, for the improvement of the postwar distribution of income over its *prewar* distribution, for its constancy over the past thirty-five years, and for the amelioration of poverty. In conjunction with macroeconomic policies, they also contributed to the greater stability of the postwar economy. In short, *the redistributive and stabilizing activities of the government have played a positive role in the postwar performance of the American economy*—with the redistributive impact largely the result of "the rapid growth of cash transfers [and] . . . the War on Poverty . . . ,[as well as] the equally rapid growth of transfers in kind, . . . [and] other programs such as affirmative action guidelines, equal opportunity and antidiscrimination laws" (p. 473).

However well we may have done in improving the distribution of income and preventing its deterioration over the postwar years, the fact remains that income is a *flow* dependent on the *stock* of wealth. What of the distribution of wealth in the United States, about which we know considerably less? The distribution of wealth is worse. Blinder cites one study, based on the same 1966 population, which found a Gini ratio of .76 for wealth compared to .43 for income distribution (p. 466). The available evidence also seems to indicate that wealth inequality is relatively stable with no trend discernible. It should be obvious that an increase in the inequality of wealth would have a marked impact on the distribution of income, particularly if government tax policies were drastically changed to favor the accumulation of wealth by the already wealthy and even more so if, at the same time, the welfare aspects of government transfer payments were subject to substantial cuts—a point that will be reinforced in our discussion of the supply-side economic policies of the Reagan administration. There is, however, more to social welfare programs, as Wilbur J. Cohen has emphasized, than Gini ratios and Lorenz-curve shifts (p. 493). There is the "larger context" of hopes and aspirations and the very *legitimation* of capitalism itself.

IV

Modern capitalism has survived as long as it has because of one unique aspect of its historical development: its flexibility and its ability to respond to changed circumstances. Unlike the Bourbons and the Romanovs, capitalism has been able to defuse potentially threatening situations and to adapt along lines that assure its continuation. It has been this enormous elasticity of capitalism, within a relatively democratic context, that has confounded vulgar Marxian analyses of capitalism's "internal contradictions," which according to a mechanical dialectic guaranteed its demise in a bloody collapse. It has been capitalism's ability to place "an iron bit in nature's mouth" that has enabled it to co-opt its opponents through higher and higher levels of real income. The key lies in a virtually limitless accumulation of capital and the growth that goes along with that accumulation. And it is growth that has served, up to now, to legitimate the capitalist system and defuse the maldistribution of income and wealth as a politically destabilizing factor. As long as growth and capital accumulation continue, distribution is not a political problem. There can be no legitimation crisis; the system is seen and accepted as just. It is only when growth becomes the "problematic" that capitalism is delegitimated and distribution repoliticized.

This is exactly what happened in the 1930s. The economic crisis was transformed into a social and political crisis with a resurfacing of class antagonism—as Britain is now experiencing in the wake of Margaret Thatcher's policies and as the United States is almost certain to experience as it follows in the same direction. The problem in the 1930s was that investment, or increases in the means of production (the physical stock of capital), was largely a private matter in which the state had no direct role to play. The government's response to the Great Depression was to try to influence investment decisions indirectly by encouraging consumer spending via personal income tax changes and transfer payments and, more directly, by trying to organize businesses into huge cartels under the NRA and by outright grants and subsidies to business via the Reconstruction Finance Corporation (RFC). The postwar growth of government was the result of these policies, with cuts in corporate income taxes, investment tax credits, and accelerated depreciation the modern and softer variations on the New Deal theme.

During the late 1950s up to the United States' involvement in the Vietnam War, the postwar performance of the economy was, as we have seen, largely successful—compared to the trauma of the 1930s. The business cycle was still with us, but brief recessions were now followed by considerably larger expansions. The cycle had been tamed, so much so that liberals were quite satisfied with themselves. Political sociologists, such as Seymour Martin Lipset and Daniel Bell, loudly proclaimed *The End of Ideology.* And only a year into his presidency, John Fitzgerald Kennedy picked up the theme in two major pronouncements. Speaking before an Economic Conference in Washington (May 21, 1962) the "liberal" President Kennedy, who had surrounded himself with prominent, "fine-tuning" Keynesians, argued that "most of the problems . . . that we now face are technical problems, are administrative problems. They are very sophisticated judgments which do not lend themselves to the great sort of 'passionate movements' which have stirred this country in the past." A month later, in his Yale University commencement address, the President elaborated on his end-of-ideology theme:

> [T]he central domestic problems of our time . . . do not relate to basic clashes of philosophy and ideology . . . . What is at stake in

our economic decisions today is not some grand warfare of rival ideologies which will sweep the country with passion but the practical management of a modern economy. What we need are not labels and cliches but more basic discussion of the sophisticated and technical questions involved in keeping a great economic machinery moving ahead . . . political labels and ideological approaches are irrelevant to the solutions.

President Kennedy's mentor, intellectual-in-residence, and occasional speech writer, the historian Arthur Schlesinger, Jr., had written an article a few years earlier for the *New York Times Magazine Section* (August 4, 1957) asking: "Where Does the Liberal Go From Here?" In it, Schlesinger described the two sources of liberalism as "the vindication of the individual against economic privation and despair, [and] the vindication of the individual against moral and spiritual frustration." He then went on to state that the vindication of the individual against privation and despair had been largely achieved in the postwar period by "the most brilliant explosion of creative social thought this country has ever seen." He was convinced that modern mixed capitalism had solved its major economic problems. All that remained was a minor mopping-up operation. The problems of yesterday had been solved in the context of today. "Few liberals," he argued, "would seriously wish today to alter the mix in our present economy." Having solved virtually all of our economic problems stemming from the 1930s, what we now needed was a "new" liberalism which would "recover [its] deeper roots in the American cultural tradition [by shifting its] focus from economics and politics to the general style and quality of our civilization." Creative spontaneity could now be let loose in an economically secure world. The problem was no longer economic unemployment but that no less terrible, though more intangible, problem of "spiritual unemployment." What this new breed of liberals must do is "to help prime the pump, not economically, but ethically." Too early for Schlesinger's and President Kennedy's metaphysics to have been set in motion, one defeated Stevensonian Democrat in the elections of 1952 was heard to lament, "The trouble is, we ran out of poor people."

To a large extent, this celebration of the status quo was reflected in the sixtieth anniversary celebration of the NBER, except for one troubling development: the 1970s. The consensus politics of the 1950s and early 1960s began unraveling with the inflationary impact of the Vietnam War generated by the guns *and* butter policies of the Johnson administration. And it was during this time that monetarism challenged the conventional wisdom of Keynesian economics with its famous restatement of the quantity theory of money. Then came a series of supply shocks that made a shambles of the Phillips curve trade-off between inflation and unemployment, and the fine-tuning nostrums of orthodox, neo-classical Kennedy-Keynesians, as well as the steady-as-you-go monetary growth rule of the monetarists. Inflation was now linked with a chronic level of unemployment that made "stagflation" the faddish neologism of our time. The supply shocks started with the worldwide crop failures of 1972, quickly followed by the devastating 1973 OPEC crisis, which had a shattering effect on growth and led to a rapid acceleration of the inflation rate. Lower GNP growth rates were now associated with still higher rates of inflation. These supply shocks were an addition to the inflationary bias built into the economy by the successful postwar stabilization policies of the government. "When an economy is made depression proof," according to Okun, "private expectations and conventions become asymmetrical, introducing an inflationary bias into the system" (Feldstein, p. 169). The underlying inflation rate of about 5 percent in the 1960s was, in retrospect, politically tolerable. Building on this basic inflation rate, the supply shocks pushed the economy into double-digit inflation at the same time that employment and economic growth were seriously depressed.

Invariably, during periods of great crisis when conventional theoretical explanations no longer serve their legitimating roles, the ground is laid for the rise of crackpots and assorted runaway ideologues with simple explanations for complex problems designed explicitly for popular appeal. This is the stuff of manipula-

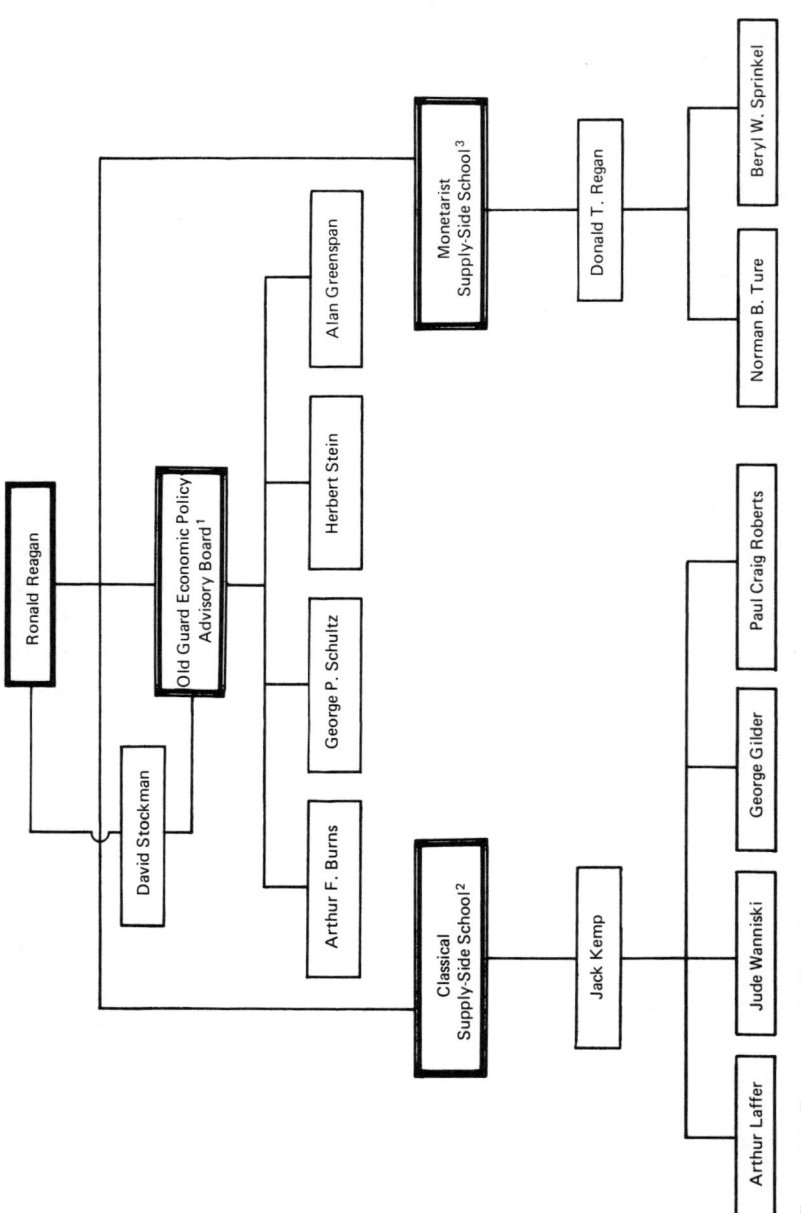

Figure 1.1. Reaganomic Genealogy

ted mass movements, particularly of a counterrevolutionary bent, where generally a single cause is attributed to all society's ills. And for single causes there are singular solutions—panaceas for piping us into the good society. It was the 1970s, and the inability of existing theories to cope with dramatic, unexpected, and unpredictable changes in the underlying structure of society, that gave rise to the ideology of supply-side economics.

V

The role of established social theory is to justify the status quo and to serve those in power. But the status quo has been shattered. We are now in the midst of a new crisis of faith, and new theories are being devised to cope with a society in disarray. It is in times such as these that a new breed of ideological visionaries emerges which is prepared to sacrifice the present along with the past in the name of a utopian future—even if it means an increase in human suffering and the sacrifice of the powerless and the disenfranchised on the way to that good society. Chiliasts have a long-run view. They are not known for their tolerance and forebearance in the short run or for their sensitivity to human suffering.

Supply-side theory is not new, nor is it revolutionary in the usual sense of that word. It is, if anything, counterrevolutionary, a desperate attempt to undo the last fifty years and to return to the prewar world of the 1920s. Supply-side theory has been lurking in the backwaters of economics for some time and would have remained there but for the election of Ronald Reagan. In those rare cases when backwater theorists gain power, they are invari-

Provenance: (1) Burns, Chairman, Council of Economic Advisors, and Chairman of the Board of Governors of the Federal Reserve System under Nixon; Schultz, Secretary of the Treasury under Nixon; Stein, Chairman of the Council of Economic Advisors under Nixon; Greenspan, Chairman of the Council of Economic Advisors under Ford: (2) Kemp, U.S. Congressman; Laffer, economist; Wanniski, formerly *Wall Street Journal*; Gilder, formerly *Wall Street Journal*; Roberts, formerly *Wall Street Journal*, economist: (3) Regan, Secretary of the Treasury under Reagan; Ture, Under Secretary of the Treasury for Tax and Economic Policy under Reagan; Sprinkel, Under Secretary of the Treasury for Monetary Affairs under Reagan.

ably corrupted by the need to consolidate that power. Praxis and theory are torn apart in the ensuing struggle. Purists demand that the "revolution" be realized in its full dimension. Pragmatists advise caution and the tempering of theory in the face of political realities. To compound the problem, the theory itself splinters into warring camps with different factions at each other's throats.

Supply-side economics is not a coherent system of intellectual thought. It is a grab bag of ill-thought-out, flaky ideas. It has within it different strains based on different ideological antecedents. It is essentially conservative, if not reactionary. It represents a return to the economic theories of the 1920s based on "free" markets. It has little to learn from history. The past is not to be studied and interpreted; it is to be molded into theoretical compliance. It is to be rewritten and undone.

Reaganomics, as distinct from supply-side economics, is a general term covering basically three loosely allied groups, each with its own particular viewpoint. The only thing that unites them is a shared aversion to the liberal policies of the postwar period. Each gives conflicting advice to the President, and each jockeys against the others in the corridors of power.

An organizational flowchart of Reaganomics is shown in Figure 1.1. There are three main groups. The first is the President's informal Economic Policy Advisory Board, consisting of Old Guard Republican conservatives who believe in cutting government expenditures and balancing the budget. Second, there is the Classical Supply-Side School under the putative leadership of Congressman Jack Kemp, but dominated by three former *Wall Street Journal* writers, two of them the authors of the two basic books on supply-side economics. For this school, tax cuts are the key to prosperity, and deficits, even if they unbalance the budget, are of secondary importance. Finally, the Monetarist Supply-Side School is to be found in the Treasury Department under Donald Regan. Norman Ture and Beryl Sprinkel are followers of the Chicago School economist Milton Friedman. For the classical school, tax cuts are everything, and monetarism is either dismissed as misguided or relegated to a secondary position. For the monetarist school, control of the money supply is the key to all problems. And for the Advisory Board, the federal budget must be balanced—at all costs.

In the chapters that follow, each of the three factions within the Reagan camp is analyzed and the tensions among them spelled out. At this writing, it is not possible to predict which of the three will ultimately dominate. The chances are that Reaganomics will ignore the contradictions and borrow from all three simultaneously in varying combinations depending on which way the political winds are blowing.

Notes

[1] Quoted in T. W. Hutchison, *A Review of Economic Doctrines, 1870-1929.* London: Oxford University Press, 1953; pp. 4-5.

[2] Martin Feldstein, ed., *The American Economy in Transition.* Chicago: University of Chicago Press, 1980. Page references of contributors to the NBER conference refer to this volume.

[3] A Lorenz curve compares the cumulative percentage of family income to the cumulative percentage of the number of families. Perfect equality (a straight-line Lorenz curve) means that 25 percent of the total number of families gets 25 percent of total family income, 50 percent of families 50 percent of income, and so on. A bowed Lorenz curve implies a less than perfect distribution of income. The Gini ratio is a measure of the area between the linear and the actual Lorenz curves as a proportion of the total area. It is therefore a numerical measure of the degree of inequality in the distribution of income. The higher the Gini ratio, the higher the degree of inequality.

CHAPTER 2

Classical Supply-Side Economics

I

The two major exponents of classical supply-side economics are Jude Wanniski and George Gilder—two journalists, self-taught in economics, who have taken on the entire profession in its current disarray. Their books? *The Way the World Works* (1979) and *Wealth and Poverty* (1981). Their sales? Enormous. Their pitch? Supply-side economics. Their mentors? Arthur Laffer, Robert Mundell, Ayn Rand, William F. Buckley, Jr., Irving Kristol, Friedrich von Hayek, Paul Craig Roberts, and (with reservations) Milton Friedman. Their disciple? Ronald Reagan.[1] Their whipping boys? John Kenneth Galbraith, Lester Thurow, and Robert Heilbroner.

These two crusaders for the wealthy and apologists for the harshest and most baneful features of capitalism have captured the popular imagination and, more importantly, that of the politicians now in power. To historians of economic thought their books will seem more Bastiat than Schumpeter, more heavily larded with an overabundance of von Mises than with the mitigating penance of Knight.

Keynesians had to wait until the 1960s to sniff at the hems of power, only to fail in the Camelot days of JFK and Vietnam. Monetarists got trapped in Goldwater's burning wagon in 1964, although later they did better in other lands with Margaret Thatcher and Augusto Pinochet. Marxism, of course, was perverted by Lenin fifty years after the fact. But classical supply-side economics has "hit the ground running," as that bandied Reagan camp saying goes.

"Progress," wrote George Santayana, "is relative to an ideal which reflection creates." "Change," said Bertrand Russell, "is indubitable. Progress is a matter of controversy." There is little "reflection" in classical supply-side economics, which, no doubt, is the reason why it has been able to reduce all "controversy" to a romantic celebration of an idealized capitalism. And if "change" has been for the worse, as these supply-siders are convinced, then we can progress only by going backward—by repealing the last half-century. We can indeed go home again, we are told, to an individualized world of work, thrift, and altruistic giving by the rich in monumental acts of noblesse oblige.

What is supply-side economics about? It is essentially a theory of growth, taxation, and fiscal policy which, if realized on its terms, renders moot the divisive problem of redistribution. Supply-side economics is capitalism writ large.

II

Supply-side economics revolves around the Laffer curve. Without it, there would be little left. It is the glue that holds classical supply-side economics together, tenuously.

Economists have been known to jot down ideas and equations on the backs of used envelopes, but classical supply-side economics started with a napkin in a Washington, D.C., restaurant, where Jude Wanniski and Arthur Laffer were having dinner with the conservative Columbia University economist Robert Mundell. The *Wall Street Journal* (October 8, 1981) has documented the momentous discovery of the Laffer curve.

> "Art was the only economist I know who would answer silly questions about economics," says Mr. Wanniski, whose college major had been in political science. One of Mr. Wanniski's first questions was: "Who is the greatest economist alive today?" Mr. Laffer's reply: Robert Mundell . . .
>
> Defying conventional economic wisdom, Mr. Mundell [in an

address he gave at a conference in Washington] argued for a tax cut, rather than a tax increase, following the surge in world oil prices in 1973. The oil-price shock would cause a recession, he predicted (accurately) and thus, he said, should be combated with a stimulative tax cut [coupled with a restrictive monetary policy to offset the tax cut's inflationary effects]. . . .

Mr. Laffer, who was in the audience, listened raptly. "It just set me off," he says. He eventually worked out a theory elaborating on Mr. Mundell's idea. The income tax, he decided, was stifling economic incentives so much that a broad-based tax cut needn't merely increase consumer spending—as "demand-side" models showed. If properly structured, a tax cut could ignite such an explosion in productive effort, he held, that the loss in Treasury revenues would be more than offset.

It was over cocktails at a Washington restaurant . . ., according to Wanniski, that Mr. Laffer first drew the now-famous Laffer curve on a napkin to illustrate his theory.

Mundell's talk "set" Laffer off and Laffer's napkin diagram "hit" Wanniski with the force of revelation. Just exactly what is the Laffer curve and what is the "theory " behind it?

The Laffer curve is essentially an extension of Alfred Marshall's nineteenth-century notion of the demand curve for a product. The area under the Marshallian demand curve is total revenue, or the quantity demanded times its price. It represents the amount that would be spent on a commodity at any given price. If a fall in price results in a more than proportionate increase in demand, total revenue (the area under the demand curve) gets larger and demand is said to be price *elastic;* that is, the percentage increase in the quantity demanded is greater than the percentage decrease in price. If the quantity demanded increases less than proportionately to the fall in price, demand is then said to be price *inelastic* and revenue falls with each decrease in price. It is a simple relationship which every undergraduate in an introductory economics course is aware of.

To connect Marshall to Laffer all one has to do is substitute the tax rate for price and taxable income for the quantity demanded.

CLASSICAL SUPPLY-SIDE ECONOMICS

If a cut in the tax rate leads to a less than proportionate increase in taxable income, the government's tax revenue will fall and revenue will be tax *inelastic*. If, on the other hand, the cut in the tax rate leads to a more than proportionate increase in taxable income, the government's tax revenue will rise and revenue will be tax *elastic*. For example, if personal taxable income is $1.5 trillion and the tax rate for the economy as a whole is 20 percent, the government's tax

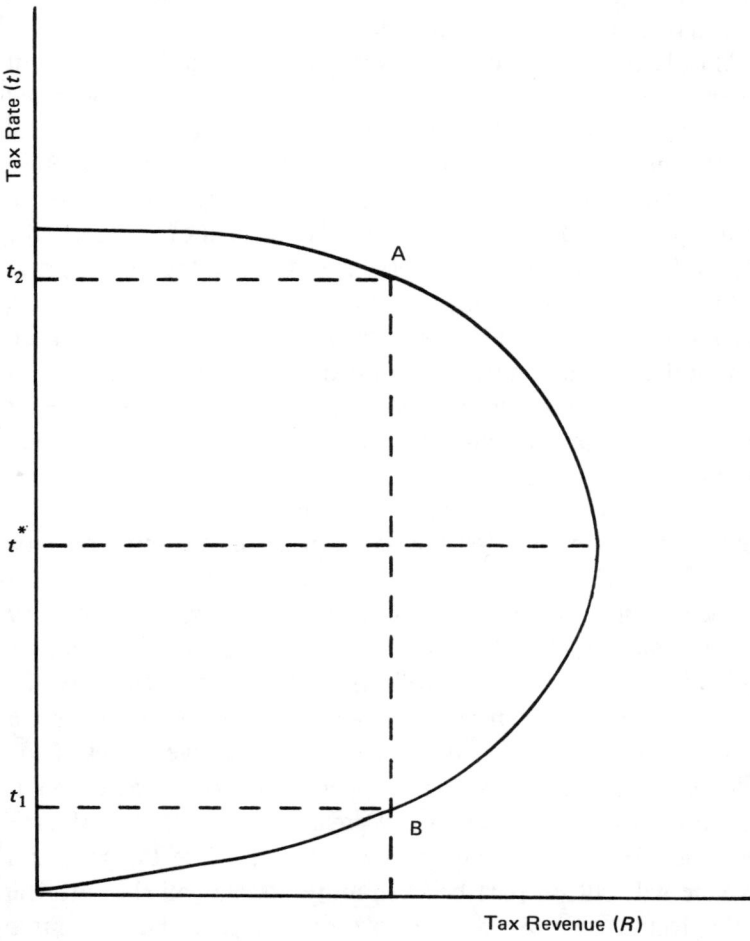

Figure 2.1. The Laffer Curve

revenue will be $300 billion. Suppose the tax rate falls to 15 percent (a reduction of 25 percent in the tax rate) and taxable income increases (however improbably) to $2.25 trillion, or by 50 percent, as a direct result solely of the tax cut. The government's tax revenue will now be $2.25 trillion × 0.15 = $340 billion or an *increase* of $40 billion. The tax elasticity (e_t) is 0.50/0.25 = 2; it is greater than 1 and therefore *elastic*. A tax *cut* has resulted in an *increase* in government revenue—an argument which plays a critical role in classical supply-side theory.

This Laffer relationship between tax rates and government revenue can be shown in the form of a curve—the celebrated *Laffer curve*. Figure 2.1 has tax rates on the vertical axis and total tax revenues on the other. On its upper, negatively sloped reaches, a *cut* in the tax rate results in a more than proportionate increase in taxable income and hence a rise in total tax revenue ($e_t > 1$). On the positively sloped portion, the effect of a *rise* in the tax rate also yields an increase in total tax revenue because of a less than proportionate decrease in taxable income ($e_t < 1$). If we keep cutting the tax rate on the upper portion of the Laffer curve and raising it on the lower portion, we will eventually reach that optimal, or *ideal*, tax rate where total tax revenue is at a maximum.

The Laffer curve therefore emerges in the shape of a distended belly with the umbilicus serving as the point of maximum revenue ($e_t = 1$ for t^*). From this peculiar curve comes the favorite litany of classical supply-side economics: *There are always two rates of taxation that produce the same revenue*—as shown by points A and B in the diagram. This follows from the very nature of the curve. What follows next is the supply-side obsession with a particular range of the Laffer curve. For any given level of tax revenue, the tax rate lying on the upper reaches of the curve (point A) represents a tax-rate elasticity greater than 1. *Reduce* the tax rate and tax revenues will *increase*. Increase the tax rate and revenue will fall, in part because more people will slip into the underground economy where no taxes are paid. For the *same* revenue level on the lower, positively sloped segment, (point B) the total revenue curve is tax inelastic ($e_t < 1$), with exactly opposite results and no underground economy to speak of, as tax payers willingly come in from out of the cold.

The tax rate, obviously, has a range between zero and 100 percent. At 100 percent, nobody would work for pay, and the government's tax take would be zero—only an underground barter economy would exist. At a zero tax rate, however, without revenues, there would be no government at all, and anarchy would reign. It would be a Rabelaisian world of *fay ce que vouldras*. We exist, therefore, somewhere between these two extremes.

The belly-button ideal, the *optimum* where revenues are at a maximum, *"is the point at which the electorate desires to be taxed."*[2] Reversing the axes, it is the North Pole of the Laffer curve: with any step in any direction revenues will fall. "It is," moreover, "the politician's job to find out what that [ideal] rate is."[3] It is not necessarily 50 percent, though it could be. It all depends on the sensibilities of taxpayers and the amount of government services they *wish* to have and are willing to pay for without coercion. And how are we to find this ideal tax rate? It's simple. "The easiest way for a political leader to determine whether an increase in the rates will produce increased rather than falling revenues is by putting the proposition to the electorate" (Wanniski, p. 100). All it would take is a referendum!

There is no doubt in the minds of classical supply-siders that we are way beyond the optimal point on the upper reaches of the Laffer curve.[4] If so, then a tax cut will result in increased revenues, with the opposite effect for a rise. The explanation lies, apart from the underground-economy effect of high taxes, in the "fact" that high taxes are associated with low levels of output, and low tax rates with high output levels—the incentive effect, as we shall see. If we are indeed on the negatively sloped portion of the Laffer curve, cutting taxes will do wonders. Empirical evidence? Warren G. Harding cut taxes after World War I and the economy boomed. Why it then collapsed in the 1930s is somewhat muted, although classical supply-side writers attribute the Great Depression *solely* to the Harley-Smoot Tariff Act of 1930—without that mistake things would have bounced along nicely at the lower tax rates then prevailing. Similarly for the Kennedy-Johnson tax cut of 1964 (eulogized by supply-siders) and the postwar tax cuts of Germany and Japan. Other factors that might have contributed to the postwar boom in the 1960s (the Vietnam War, for one) are blithely ignored. Seek and ye shall find. Proof consists in combing history (back to Alexander the Great) and picking out simple historical illustrations that serve your theory. Other heroes in the supply-side pantheon are Andrew Mellon, Calvin Coolidge, Ludwig Erhard, and Governor Carlos Romero Barcelo of Puerto Rico—all true tax-cut believers, the latter having saved his commonwealth "when," according to Gilder, he "was so fortunate as to meet Arthur Laffer" in the late 1970s.[5] My favorite quotation, however, is from quarterback Jack Kemp (p. 46). His "proof" that we are on the upper reaches of the Laffer curve is as charmingly pure as open receivers on the gridiron. "When you look around and see so much evidence of unemployment and underemployment. . . . When you see more and more people shifting out of work . . . you sense that the rates are too high, and you don't have to consult a professional economist to know that lower rates would be healthier for the economy [by increasing real output] and would be likely to produce greater revenues [as a result]." Clearly, there is no such thing as involuntary unemployment.

*Post*diction in support on one's theory is easy; *pre*diction is another matter. The following quotation from Wanniski leaps off the page (p. 298, italics supplied):

> At this writing, in the autumn of 1977, Britain's Conservative Party leader Margaret Thatcher is steadfastly pledging to sharply reduce the progressivity of Britain's personal tax rates as soon as her party returns to power. . . . *Once Britain takes this step,* the expansion of its economy will have rippling effects through Western Europe, giving courage to conservative coalitions in other capitals to follow her lead.

Well, Margaret Thatcher won, and at *this* writing in the spring of 1982 the British economy is in the worst state since the Great

Depression, with a disastrous growth rate, unemployment at over 12 percent, and riots in the streets across the breadth of England last summer. One historical illustration is as good as another, although I would not maintain that Margaret Thatcher disproves supply-side theory any more than I would accept that Wanniski's, Gilder's, and Kemp's illustrations prove it. History is messy, refusing to yield its secrets clearly except to simple or desperate minds. Supply-siders should be forced to repeat, every hour on the hour, that old Jewish proverb: *For example is not a proof!*

III

Classical supply-side economists believe that a tax cut will increase government revenues by inducing an increase in real output. Why? What lies behind the Laffer curve? To begin with, it must be stressed that the Laffer curve refers exclusively to the progressive personal income tax. For fiscal year 1980 (October 1-September 30), the total domestic tax receipts of the federal government amounted to $500 billion. Of this total, the federal government realized $244 billion (49 percent) from individual income taxes; $161 billion (32 percent) from Social Security taxes; $65 billion (13 percent) from corporate income taxes; $24 billion (5 percent) from excise taxes; and $6 billion (1 percent) from estate and gift taxes. Of the government's total domestic tax receipts, less than one-half came from personal income taxes and over half from all other sources. Personal income taxes consist of taxes on earned income (wages and salaries), income from investments, and capital gains. It is to these types of taxes that the Laffer curve applies, and not to corporate income or excise taxes (estate and gift taxes being insignificant, even more so after the 1981 tax bill of the Reagan administration which virtually did away with them). The Laffer curve therefore applies to considerably less than the total tax receipts of the federal government.

The output effect of tax cuts in supply-side economics is, then, restricted to taxes on the personal income of *individuals,* which account for only a portion of the government's tax receipts. But why, according to supply-side "theorists," is the output response of such a magnitude as to result in an *increase* in tax revenues? Why does it lead to a more than proportionate increase in taxable income? Why, in other words, are we on the upper, negatively sloped reaches of the Laffer curve where revenue is tax elastic? The answer is the *marginal* tax rate, that is, the progressive increase in the tax rate which is applied to each *increment* of income as the individual is pushed up into higher and higher brackets with each increase in his nominal income. Prior to the Reagan tax cut, the maximum tax was 50 percent on earned income, 70 percent on investment income (interest, dividends, and rents) and 28 percent on capital gains.[6] The next question is: Why would a cut in the *marginal* tax rates have such a remarkable effect on output and taxable income? The answer lies in a convenient theory of human behavior which converts supply-side economics into a theory of growth, where growth is a unique function of the marginal tax rate and its pronounced effect on the motivations of *individuals*.

To start with, we are told by Jude Wanniski that everything affects everything else in a general equilibrium model.[7] In Wanniski's immortal words, *"Jump up and down and the whole world shakes a bit"* (p. 19, italics supplied). Or, as French wit would have it: *Tout est dans tout, et réciproquement!* The margin is the key to it all. "Very few people *think* on the margin, but everyone *acts* on the margin" (p. 43, original italics). Even children! "By the time children are three or four years old," we are told, "they have acquired such a body of information by studying tax schedules and their variables within the family that they can consciously 'think on the margin' " (p. 47). And when they grow up and earn their own money they become obsessed with the real marginal tax rates of the adult world—so much so that their behavior is dominated by it. And since economic growth is the result of human behavior and the psychological laws that govern it, it is uniquely dependent on the level of the marginal tax rate. An open and shut case for Wanniski.

To Wanniski there is physical capital and there is *intellectual* capital. The personal income marginal tax rates are a tax on intellectual capital, while the corporate income tax is a tax on profits, not on the physical capital itself. Government, in other words, has a bias against intellectual capital which affects the incentive to work. "People," says Wanniski, "work for one reason and one reason only: to maximize their welfare" (p.71). There are, of course, certain "minimum necessities for survival—food, clothing, shelter, etc." But after satisfying them, "the individual is free to choose between work and leisure." Given an individual's "personal assessment of what constitutes welfare," he will "work *up to [that] point* and then not work" (p. 71, original italics). People "only work to improve their welfare" (p. 91).

This brings up the much-touted *wedge model* of Lafferian theory. It is government, through its power to tax, that introduces a "wedge" between what one gets for working and what one is allowed to keep. Personal income and social security taxes, however, are only one part of the wedge. So are minimum wage laws, taxes on capital, tariffs, all forms of government regulation, nonwork subsidies such as welfare entitlements, and anything else that represents "government intervention in private transactions" (p. 84). But the marginal rates of the personal income tax, which ranged until recently from 14 to 70 percent, are the single greatest source of disincentive insofar as the Lafferite supply-siders are concerned. In Laffer's words:

> Marginal taxes [tax rates] . . . stand as a wedge between what an employer pays his factors of production and what they ultimately receive in after-tax income. . . . *In order to increase total output,* policy measures must have the effect of both increasing firms' demand for productive factors and *increasing the productive factors' desire to be employed.* Taxes of all sorts must be reduced. These reductions will be most effective where they lower *marginal* tax rates the most. Any reduction in marginal rates means that the employer will pay less and yet employees will receive more. Both from the employer and employee point of view *more employment will be desired and more output will be forthcoming.*[8]

This is a neoclassical labor market humming along under Keynes's Postulates I and II if there ever was one[9]—*one in which all unemployment is voluntary.* Not to be outdone, Gilder is even more explicit. "It is marginal tax rates," he writes, "that determine the impact of a tax on motives and . . . on the willingness to go out and work," and these same high marginal tax rates "continuously undermine the very diligence and determination that are necessary to accomplish any useful work in the world."[10]

My all-time too-good-not-to-be-quoted gem comes from Wanniski:

> [In] comes Mary S., with every intention of trying to get a job at the Metropolitan Opera, perhaps in the chorus, and to work her way to stardom [shades of *42nd Street!*]. If she can't make it in this endeavor, she will become a prostitute. Upon arriving, she learns that the government has just introduced a wedge of 33 percent at the Metropolitan Opera, and it is now relatively more profitable to be a prostitute. Equilibrium is restored on the supply-side of this process when so many women become prostitutes that each has to put in 33 percent more time in pursuit of business. *It is clear that an increase in the government wedge decreases the quality of opera and increases the supply of prostitutes* (p. 94, italics supplied.)[11]

Still, Wanniski notwithstanding, there is some hope for Mary S. A pimp's wedge cuts wider than the government's 33 percent. But Wanniski holds out another kind of hope for poor Mary S.

> In the larger economy, it is of course unlikely that Mary S., the potential opera star, is directly shifted into an underworld occupation. Rather she shifts into a lesser occupation, becoming "underemployed" in the money economy, and the wedge concurrently shifts all other employees downward into the underemployment classes, where *at the margin* an aspiring shopperson is the one who actually goes over the edge into bartering via prostitution (footnote, p. 94-95, italics supplied).

What a pity! The margin at its malevolent worst! How much better it would be to have prostitutes capable of trilling Mozart arias on the job. Think what it could do for the cultural uplifting of a prostitute's clientele. Clearly the margin and "the expanding wedge" are capable of all sorts of wicked things.

At this point it might be wise to turn to George Gilder's book, which one *noblesse de robe* supply-sider found "Promethean in its intellectual power and insight."[12] I found it breathless.

IV

Gilder's book is about "the high adventure and redemptive morality of capitalism. (p. x)" Early on he proclaims the *golden rule* of capitalism: "The belief that the good fortune of others is also finally one's own" (p. 9), particularly the "good fortune" of the upper classes who are "the cutting edge of the economy—the source of most investment" (p. 20). When the capitalist elite are demoralized, it is the poor who suffer most, and nothing demoralizes capitalists more than high marginal tax rates whose proceeds are used to finance the welfare state in grandiose redistribution schemes—Roosevelt's New Deal and L. B. Johnson's War on Poverty being the prime examples of the compassionate heart gone wrong. Take care of the poor and the vitality is sapped out of the capitalist elite, which serves only to make the poor more hapless after the inevitable decline in output.

It is the capitalist elite, as owners of the factors of production other than labor, who are exposed to risk in an uncertain world. When they add to the stock of capital, they have no assurance of new revenue. They take the plunge on faith. They are altruistic *givers*. They *are* the supply side. They "give in order to get" without being sure of the getting. They "supply in order to demand" (p. 28).[13]

It is the welfare state operating on the demand side that cripples the supply side and results in "a sluggish and uncreative economy" (p. 29). "Egalitarianism in the economy," we are told, "tends to promote greed" (p. 30) in the mob. And when, in a plebiscitarian mobocracy, "mass sentiment" is allowed "to dictate to the powerful and permanent mechanisms of representative leadership[,] [t]he result is a restive and alienated electorate, a failure of political authority, . . . and a tendency toward national decline" (p. 29). The very vibrancy of capitalism "depends not on automatic mechanisms [Gilder has little use for the perfect competition model which is itself egalitarian], but on the quality, creativity, and leadership of the capitalists" (p. 38). Gilder is an out-and-out elitist:

> [L]eadership is supply and public opinion is demand.
>
> . . . .
>
> [L]eaders, to the extent that they bear real authority, tend to create the views of the larger constituencies more than they follow them [p. 29].
>
> . . . .
>
> [S]uccessful politicians are engaged not in passive response to public demand, but in the active supply and marketing of ideas. *Supply can create its own demand, even in the political realm* [p. 29, italics supplied].
>
> . . . .
>
> The will of the people is often no more "spontaneous" or free of elite initiative and manipulation in politics than in economics. Democratic masses cannot be generative or creative; they can merely react and ratify [p. 38].

It is by the "experimental competition of elites" (p. 38) that capitalism generates its dynamism. It is a boiling cauldron of great convection currents within which the natural elite rise to the top, and the tired, worn-out elite, having done their thing, are cast down from whence they came. It is a rampant social and economic Darwinism, with elitist liberal arts colleges and universities guaranteeing the downward mobility of the effete children of the upper classes (those "humpty-dumpty heirs of wealth"-p. 61) to make way for the blueing of America. Look at Ronald Reagan and that millionaires' club called the U.S. Senate, most of whose members are self-made men, not to mention the president of Mobil Oil, the son of a Greek socialist immigrant peasant.[14] "Material progress," Gilder tells us, "is ineluctably elitist: it makes the rich richer and increases their number, exalting the few extraordinary men who can produce wealth over the democratic masses who consume it. . . . *Material progress, although democratically demanded, is procedurally undemocratic*" (p. 259, italics supplied).

And it is the welfare state's coddling of the poor that keeps them from participating in the economy by sapping their incentive to work and to improve their own lot by their own efforts. They have been turned, to use "Engine Charlie" Wilson's felicitous metaphor, into kennel dogs sitting on their haunches yapping for the next handout, not hunting dogs alert and lean of muscle foraging for their food.

The textbook case of perfect competition, moreover, "has little to do with the central activity of capitalism, which is the turbulent process of launching new enterprise. . . . Perfect competition . . . excludes most supply-side behavior," since in equilibrium firms "can essentially affect neither supply nor demand" (p. 31). The very foundation of supply-side economics is that "producers, collectively, in the course of production, create demand for their goods" (p. 32). They are not kennel-dog "takers" of what the market gives them.

Capitalism's go-go people are the *very* rich. And it is not the role of the rich to "titillate the classes below, but to invest" (p. 62). The rich, unlike the poor, consume a small proportion of their income—except when high marginal tax rates and bracket creep force them to pour their millions into sinkholes: tax shelters and collectibles (gold, art, precious stones, etc.) that add nothing to productive capacity. "A successful economy depends on the proliferation of the rich" (p. 245) unfettered by the government and protected from the masses who push misguided liberal politicians into counterproductive redistributive welfare boondoggles.

Since the poor eat what they get and do not save by the very nature of their circumstances, and the rich cannot possibly eat all of what they get and save the rest, and since it is our tax structure that has sapped the vitality of capitalism, let the government use its tax powers *to redistribute income in favor of the rich*. This would, of course, require the cutting of welfare programs in order to force the poor to work for their own benefit and moral improvement.

Past redistribution efforts in favor of the poor have only served, according to supply-side ideology, to decrease incentives to work, by rich *and* poor. These efforts have therefore decreased investment, productivity, and growth. The visible effects are increased unemployment, inflation, underground economic activity, tax shelters, and other sinkholes for the rich and, contrary to expectations, an increase in the level of poverty.

The poor can be helped only by stimulating saving and investment, which can be achieved only by skewing the distribution of income in favor of the well to do. The poor do not choose not to work because of "moral weakness, but because they are paid [not] to do so" by welfare and subsidy programs (p. 68). Indeed, the welfare state has raised the marginal tax rate for the poor to the 100 percent level, or so the argument goes, trapping them into their dependency by making work unprofitable. Moreover, the male poor have been "cuckolded by the compassionate state" (p. 115) and driven out of the family unit, their own macho self-image shattered.

What we need do to help the poor is to change our tax structure radically—to make it less progressive by a greater use of *regressive* taxes, for, Gilder tells us, *"regressive taxes help the poor"* (p. 188). The argument is as simple as it is simple-minded. Gilder writes:

> It has become increasingly obvious that a less progressive tax structure is necessary to reduce the tax burden on the lower and

middle classes. When rates are lowered *in the top brackets,* the rich consume less and invest more. Their earnings rise and *they pay more taxes in absolute amounts.* Thus the lower and middle classes need pay less to sustain a given level of government services. . . . [T]o help the poor and middle classes, one must cut the tax rates of the rich (p. 188, italics supplied).

An ingenious argument: the cut in taxes on the rich will so stimulate output that the tax revenue increases from the rich alone will allow tax cuts for the low- and middle-income classes.[15] Once upon a time it used to be argued, to counter Marxists, that taxing the rich more would not generate enough additional revenue to help the poor because the poor are many and the rich few. Supply-siders add that, regardless of their fewness, taxing the rich to *help* the poor serves only to reduce output, thus worsening the condition of the poor. Now the argument is that, no matter how few the rich are, cutting *their* taxes will increase *their* pretax incomes to such an extent that government coffers will overflow, more than just compensating for the smallness of their number. Gilder's supply-side argument is a growth argument, which states that productive activity is powerfully dependent on the after-tax income of the venturesome rich, who alone are the dynamic growth force in a capitalist society and thus entitled to a skewing of taxes in their favor.

The growth aspect of the argument has not escaped Jack Kemp. Borrowing from a JFK speech, his leitmotif is: *A rising tide lifts all boats.* If factional strife and class struggle are to be avoided, growth must accelerate. Again, it is "the rich and powerful and creative—*a group relatively small in number*—[who] are ready to pull, if only they are not discouraged by government from doing so" (p. 31, italics supplied). And "the tax system [is] the key to spurring real economic growth" (p. 37). High taxes, especially on the rich, "impoverish the community at large." Robert Mundell is brought in to clinch the argument: "The level of U.S. taxes has become a drag on economic growth in the United States. The national economy is being choked by taxes—asphyxiated" (quoted in Kemp, p. 37)—to which Kemp adds: "Tax relief is not so much an end in itself as a means of getting this economy moving again. Economic growth must come first" (p. 49). Then, of course, quarterback Kemp is an ardent Laffer curve team player. Cut taxes and revenues and growth will increase. Kemp would like to see the maximum marginal tax rate reduced to 25 percent. That should do it. A "growth-oriented tax policy [would] increase the tax base by increasing the volume of work, saving, and investment" (p. 102).[16]

V

Supply-siders know what causes unemployment: high taxes on the rich which prevent the economy from rolling along at its full-employment potential. They also know what causes inflation: *taxes*. Since taxes simultaneously cause unemployment and inflation, supply-siders also have a theory of "stagflation," and a cure for it: cut taxes.

Borrowing from Paul Craig Roberts, a most solemn and unbending missionary, Gilder claims that high taxes act as a brake on production and that this *tax brake* causes inflation by reducing the supply of goods. Inflation is neither demand-pull nor cost-push. It is *tax-push* in that taxes "have an immediately inflationary impact on wages and prices" (p. 193). Gilder's theory of inflation is based on a markup theory of pricing. The base price of any marketable good is "the sum of . . . intermediate costs plus a share of *other costs passed on in its price"* (p. 202, italics supplied). The costs of the welfare state induce higher taxes, whether outright or by bracket creep. And since "all final prices embody the pyramid of public services, paid for by taxes at every point in the productive system," there is a *"diffusion* through the price structure of the rising costs of government" (p. 203, original italics).[17] It follows, therefore, that "government, with its ever-proliferating . . . services and inefficiencies" (p. 203), is the chief cause of inflation. Taxes push up prices which then cause wages to rise and so on into the spiral. Inflation is tax-push inflation, where tax increases are used to finance an expanding welfare state.

Gilder is uncompromising: "Inflation is caused by taxes" (p. 190), not by increases in the money supply. Gilder is one supply-sider who has virtually no use for Milton Friedman and his monetarist epigones. "[I]t is self-destructive for conservatives to pretend that the inflationary impact of taxes on costs is chiefly a problem of the money supply" (p. 204). (It is not.) What is needed is to "economize on [government]." Prices are a function of government taxes, not the money supply. Gilder's rejection of Friedman is unequivocal—Friedman is a demand-sider, a variation on a Keynesian theme. In the first place, Friedman got it all wrong. He did not support the Kemp-Roth bill for its supply-side effect but "only because it would exert pressures for cuts in spending" (p. 191). He failed to realize that the effect of the proposed Kemp-Roth bill is "on business creativity and investment" (p. 191), i.e., the supply side.

Furthermore, monetarists cannot easily define the money supply or control it "during periods of rapid economic change" (p. 195), and there is no historical evidence "that any particular level of money supply is uniquely favorable to economic health" (p. 202). Restricting the money supply to fight inflation can only serve to "dampen private-sector growth," which alone is "the best way to fight inflation" (p. 202). "To say that the Federal Reserve should not accommodate government spending is, in practice, to say that business should pay" (p. 204). Moreover, "any attempt to fight inflation by monetary contraction alone at a time of repeated shocks to supply will cause new, yet more destructive, and more permanent inflation" (p. 205). And to make sure we get the message, we have the following (p. 205, italics supplied): *"There is no practicable antiinflationary program except Lafferite economics and supply-side stimuli."*

The quantity theory of money has a fatal flaw: it emphasizes the demand side and fails to realize that the money supply is *passive,* that it automatically adjusts to the needs of trade. If "taxflation" is the explanation of inflation, then the money supply must and will expand to accommodate the higher levels of nominal GNP. To try to restrain it will only play havoc with the economy. Monetarists, like all other demand-siders, are misguided. They do not understand that "the expanding money supply . . . makes it possible for private activity to continue despite the massive diffusion of taxes" (p. 205). In short, "the generation of the demand for money [takes place] through the production of goods: the supplies that create the need for a store of value and a medium of exchange" (p. 218). Then in short bursts we get the following:

> No monetary policy can stop people from bidding up the real prices of a declining store of goods in an economy that is running down . . . [p. 218].

....

The long-run answer to the Keynesian [and monetarist] concern with aggregate demand is not a concern with the money supply, which is another facet of aggregate demand. *The answer is an unremitting cultivation of the supply of new goods*—the source of creativity and expectation *that create the demand for money* [p. 218, italics supplied].

....

[M]onetary and fiscal prodigality—deficit spending and money creation—is only the proximate cause of inflation. . . . *[I]t is not altogether regrettable at a time of steadily rising taxes* [p. 219, italics supplied].

....

[A] rigorously antiinflationary monetary policy would hurt small but rising companies more [which to Gilder are "the cutting edge" (p. 20) of capitalism], since they stand at the end of the credit queue. It is new business that suffers most when lendable funds decline [p. 223]. *[A] monetarist attack on inflation . . . will likely not affect inflation as much as it will hurt legitimate business* [p. 224, italics supplied].

And to drive the last nail into Friedman's coffin, we have: "The money supply is . . . elusive. New forms of money and credit proliferate in the United States" (p. 226), making the money supply "enormously elastic" (p. 226). The banking principle triumphs over the currency principle. And so, an end to Milton Friedman, a millstone around the neck of Gilder's New Right.

Other supply-siders, however, give increases in the money supply primacy in explaining the *initial* onslaught of price increases, with taxes serving to exacerbate an already existing inflation. To Wanniski inflation is caused, initially, by increases in the money supply in excess of the real rate of growth. When the quantity theory of money is wedded to Laffer's wedge, we get a different supply-side theory of inflation.

Wanniski notes two kinds of taxes: specific taxes and ad valorem taxes. Since specific taxes (which are generally regressive) are levied on "weight, volume, or specific activity (p. 113)," and not value, the Laffer wedge lessens with a monetarist-induced inflation. "All transactors in the economy suddenly feel a lightening of the tax wedge *after the initial turbulence of the monetary expansion* . . . [and] the economy enjoys a genuine expansion" (p. 113-114, italics supplied). Ad valorem taxes, which are in *proportion* to value, leave the Laffer wedge unaffected. But *progressive* ad valorem taxes widen the wedge, and the economy contracts as a result. In short, if excessive increases in the money supply lead to corresponding price level changes, and the wedge widens because the progressivity of the tax system (bracket creep, even if tax schedules are unchanged) causes a fall in real output (the incentive effect of supply-side economics), then we are confronted with the simultaneity of inflation and unemployment—*stagflation.*

To Jack Kemp "wages, profits, and prices no more cause inflation than wet streets cause rain" (p. 101). To fight inflation the money supply must be brought under control and taxes cut to induce antiinflationary increases in output (again, the supply-side incentive effect). Kemp, moreover, proposes to control the price level by returning to a strict gold standard. "With a restoration of dollar convertibility into some commodity of value [gold], *inflation . . . would be stopped dead in its tracks*" (p. 114). (When I read or listen to Jack Kemp, I find myself compulsively humming that popular country western song "Dropkick Me Jesus Through the Goal Posts of Life.") Obviously, supply-siders are all over the inflation map. They have to clean up their act. For the moment, we leave them wallowing in their confusion.

There is one final mystic bit of outstanding supply-side business: *the savings ratio*. Supply-siders have made much of the low ratio of savings to GNP in the United States, contrasting it unfavorably with the current two favorites—Germany and Japan—while conveniently ignoring the disparate postwar defense spending ratios. Supply-side wisdom attributes the low U.S. savings ratio to the high marginal rates of taxation, of course. Cutting them will restore savings to their proper level and induce the investment needed for an increase in supply. At the same time, the tax cuts will also call forth a greater work effort on the part of the rich and the not-so-rich—though not of the poor whose marginal tax rates, because of a perverse welfare system, are at the 100 percent level.

On the issue of work effort, higher after-tax returns for individuals could just as well cause *less* work effort in favor of more leisure time. Also, there is no guarantee that investment, as a result of a greater after-tax business income, would increase. Bountiful corporate cash flows could well lead to corporate mergers instead of new investment—as brilliantly exemplified by the recent behavior of oil companies. But perhaps the most serious cause for doubt is the cocksure, simpleminded relationship assumed between saving and the marginal tax rate. It all hinges on whether individual and business saving is dominated by *stock* goals or *flow* goals—on whether savings are destined for specific purposes or are conceived as a *proportion* of disposable income.

"Economists," argues Robert Eisner,[18] "are far from agreed that higher after-tax yields have much effect on savings or even a direct effect. To the extent people save in order to have spending power at a future time, such as retirement, lower returns make it necessary to save more" (p. 16). Moreover, adds Eisner, "there is relatively little sound evidence that the rate of return on saving has much to do with total saving" (p. 10). To Eisner, "the single greatest encouragement we can give to saving and investment . . . is to see to it that people can make choices in business and make their decisions *in a climate of prosperity and full employment"* (p. 9, italics supplied). Accordingly, government policy would be better directed to that most serious market failure in capitalist society—"the market failure of unemployment" (p. 18).

Keynesians of either the conservative-liberal or more radical Post Keynesian stripe would agree with this assessment. And so would François Mitterand. Ronald Reagan takes his place alongside Margaret Thatcher.

Classical supply-side economics suffers from an acute tax-cut fetishism. Tax cuts have become an object of irrational reverence. Some people bay at the moon, others worship the sun by cooking themselves in it, and still others burn incense and practice the black arts. For supply-siders their hangup is taxes. They can't help it. Taxes cause *all* our troubles, and tax cuts will solve everything—especially if tilted toward the rich. It is because of the *poverty of wealth,* in the sense that the rich are prevented by government from being richer still, that the poor are poorer than need be. Or, as John Kenneth Galbraith has felicitously put it, the poor won't work because they have too much money and the rich won't work because they have too little! That nicely nails the absurdity of it all.

There is, however, another sense in which a poverty of wealth exists, and that is in the intellectual poverty of classical supply-side ideas. They are the reductio ad absurdum of capitalism. Vulgar apologists for the worst features of capitalism are trying hard to make vulgar Marxism true.

Notes

[1] When the Chairman of the Senate Finance Committee, Robert Dole, was hospitalized shortly after the inauguration, President Reagan paid him a courtesy visit. Instead of flowers, he gave him a copy of Gilder's book. The Senator recovered.

[2] Jude Wanniski, *The Way the World Works*. New York: Simon and Schuster, 1979; p. 98, original italics.

[3] Jack Kemp, *An American Renaissance: A Strategy for the 1980s*. New York: Harper and Row, 1979; p. 51.

[4] Of course, benighted Keynesians and their first-cousin monetarists suffer from the delusion of thinking that we are on the lower, tax-inelastic portion, where a cut in taxes would result in a fall in the government's tax revenue.

[5] George Gilder, *Wealth and Poverty*. New York: Basic Books, 1981; p. 186. Wanniski was also a consultant to Barcelo. Indeed, he tells us that *The Way the World Works* "was written as a direct result of a trip to Puerto Rico in March, 1976" (p. 276). Apparently, the 60 percent welfare and food stamp economy in Puerto Rico is a Horatio Alger story. In a private communication, Sidney Weintraub pointed out that Puerto Rico is still an LDC surviving on welfare checks and that its industrialization came from a Puerto Rican tax *exemption* (the IRS does not apply there) and an open U.S. mainland market. If *everyone*—the full country—cut taxes in the same way, he argued, it would be a disaster for Puerto Rico. Its advantage would vanish. Weintraub's prediction has been well borne out. Only a year into the Reagan administration's economic game plan, the Puerto Rican economy, which has had a long dependence on federal transfer payments, is reeling. Some social programs have been cut by about a third, and the cut in food stamps, which affects one half of all Puerto Rican families, has been particularly hard. Unemployment has soared to nearly 30 percent of the labor force, and crime has become a serious problem. The Reagan administration's cuts in mainland business taxes has seriously eroded the "Operation Bootstrap" tax exemptions for U.S. companies investing in Puerto Rico and fiscal investment has dropped significantly. The threat now is a mass exodus to the mainland. (See *Wall Street Journal,* February 3, 1982.)

[6] The Reagan administration's 1981 tax bill reduced marginal tax rates across the board over a three-year period—5 percent, October 1, 1981; 10 percent, July 1, 1982; and 10 percent, July 1, 1983—but kept the maximum tax rate at 50 percent of *earned* income (wages and salaries), with the tax rate at the lower end reduced from 14 to 10 percent. More significantly, the top tax rate on investment income (interest, dividends, and rents) was cut from 70 to 50 percent *effective January 1,*

1982 (David Stockman's "Trojan horse"), thereby also reducing the effective capital gains tax, set back to June 10, 1981, from a maximum of 28 percent to 20 percent. The biggest tax cut is therefore going to the rich and much more quickly than for everyone else. The implications for the distributions of wealth and income are enormous. In anticipation of the argument to follow, it should be emphasized that for supply-siders the marginal tax rate is far more important than the average tax rate. A cut in the average tax rate alone would result only in a loss of tax revenue with little effect on the willingness to work and thus on real output.

[7]*How the World Works,* p. 19.

[8]Memorandum, November 1974, to the then U.S. Secretary of the Treasury, William Simon, quoted in Wanniski, pp. 85-86, italics supplied.

[9]Postulates I and II in Keynes's *General Theory* referred to the two key postulates in classical theory—that the negatively sloped demand *and* positively sloped supply of labor curves both depend on the level of real wages (nominal wages deflated by the price level, i.e., their real purchasing power)—which made involuntary unemployment in a market-dominated economy impossible. Keynes rejected the second postulate (that the supply of labor is positively related to real wages) and accepted the first—causing unnecessary trouble and confusion in the process. In classical supply-side "theory," the same result is obtained by substituting after-tax income for real wages as the independent variable in the demand and supply curves of labor. With involuntary unemployment theoretically inadmissable, the flexibility of factor and commodity prices guarantee that the economy has a unique equilibrium point at full employment, with any lapses from such an ideal state of affairs temporary and quickly corrected by the automatic forces of the market system.

[10]*Wealth and Poverty,* pp. 181, 185.

[11]At this point Laffer's tribute to Jude Wanniski's *The Way the World Works* should be indelibly recorded: "In all honesty, I believe it is the best book on economics *ever* written" [italics supplied]. George Gilder calls it "one of the great inspirational works of economic literature." George Gilder, by the way, has a Norwegian elkhound called "Laffer," whose tail faithfully reproduces the "Curve."

[12]Blurb by David Stockman, Director of the Office of Management and Budget. They really do scratch each other's backs, these supply-siders, at least until they defect and start throwing thunderbolts at each other.

[13]On reading the first draft of Chapter 4 on "The Supply Side," Gilder's wife, a

Vassar graduate, cried; she couldn't understand it. Gilder tried again. She cried again (*New York Times,* April 26, 1981). Chapter 4 now has the following footnote at the very beginning: "This is a chapter on the theory of supply-side economics, which may be safely passed over by readers who prefer a less abstract exposition of the subject." So much for a Vassar education!

[14]It would, of course, be impolite to mention the exception of David Rockefeller, Gilder's benefactor, who staked him to an education at Exeter where he finished last in his class and still got into Harvard, the alma mater of his father and David Rockefeller. He didn't do too well there either (*New York Times,* April 26, 1981).

[15]Gilder misses the point, in support of his own argument, that the incomes of the middle class, at least, will also increase (through the multiplier) leading to a secondary rise in tax revenues.

[16]It occurs to me, though it has not to any supply-siders I know of, that there is a better way to achieve their goals than through cuts in the marginal tax rates—which are politically difficult to do to an appropriate degree (the Reagan administration has cut the marginal tax rate from 70 to only 50 percent, which is still twice that which Kemp thinks is required) and even if done are too easily reversed in the next election. A better way would be a constitutional amendment (a popular ploy these days) to deny the vote to the nonpropertied classes (as some of the founding fathers wished) and to the idle, nonproductive rich living on their inheritances. This disenfranchisement would serve as a spur for the "humpty-dumpty heirs" of the rich to climb down from their walls and avail us of their creative talents by reentering the real economy—though adequate inheritances would be allowed so as not to sap the incentives of the *working* rich to provide for their degenerate progeny. Family feelings run strong among the rich; they have not been sapped by welfare handouts, at least not the kind the poor get. Still another approach would be a profit-sharing program with the working class, in lieu of tax cuts for the rich, which would equally increase work incentives and restrain wage increases. But this is unlikely to appeal to supply-siders. Given Gilder's enamorment of elites, disenfranchisement is the better bet.

[17]Although this has all the markings of a cost-push theory, Gilder apparently prefers tax-push, I suppose, on the grounds that taxes are not a *market* cost.

[18]*Savings and Economic Growth.* Hearings before the Joint Economic Committee, Congress of the United States, Ninety-Sixth Congress, Second Session, July 30, 1980.

CHAPTER 3

Demand-Side Economics*

I

In preparation for the monetarist version of supply-side economics, the orthodox quantity theory of money will be briefly outlined and compared with prevailing demand-side theories of our time, namely, the Keynesian theory of output and employment and Milton Friedman's variation on the same theme. The exposition, though necessarily sketchy and overly simplified, will serve as background for the chapters to follow.

The traditional quantity theory of money has a long history going back, at least, to the eighteenth and nineteenth centuries. It states that the total output of goods and services produced in an economy, within any given period of time (for example, one year), can be expressed in two equivalent ways. From the "goods" side, total nominal output (Y) is simply the sum of all goods produced in that period multiplied by their respective market prices, i.e., $Y = PQ$, where Q is the total real output of goods and services and P is the general price level consisting of the set of individual prices relevant to the myriad components of Q. Alternatively, from the "money" side, this is equivalent to the aggregate money supply (M) multiplied by the average number of times each unit of money turns over in a year's time, i.e., the income velocity of money (V).

―――――――――
*Following the example of Gilder, we note that the reader may skip over this chapter. Although it would help, it is not absolutely essential for understanding the remaining chapters of this book. It does serve, however, to link the two basic schools of supply-side economics and to make clearer the foundations of the monetarist supply-side school described in Chapter 4.

In short, $Y = MV$. If $Y = PQ$ and $Y = MV$, then it follows that
$$MV = PQ$$
This is the *quantity equation of exchange*. It is a tautology that describes two sides of the same coin. Clearly, if the total stock of money is $500 billion and each dollar turns over, on the average, 6 times a year, then national income is 500 × 6 or $3 trillion—which is another way of describing the total amount of real output in nominal terms, where each unit of real output is valued at its respective market price.

The quantity equation of exchange can be transformed into the *quantity theory of money* by introducing two behavioral assumptions plus a causal arrow. First, it is assumed that in a perfectly competitive market system real output in the long run is always at full employment. Short-run deviations from full employment can only be temporary; they are quickly corrected by the automatic forces of the market system. For all intents and purposes, therefore, Q can be taken as given. Next, the rate of turnover of the money supply is determined by the institutional arrangements of the financial system. The underlying financial structure of the economy, it is assumed, changes very slowly over the secular long run. Therefore, V can also be taken as given. With Q and V given, the theory now states that a one-way causal arrow exists which indicates that prices (P) respond to changes in the money supply (M), *not* the other way around. Our equation becomes:

$$M \overset{\rightarrow}{=} P \left(\frac{\bar{Q}}{\bar{V}} \right) \qquad \text{or} \qquad P \overset{\leftarrow}{=} f(M)$$

with the causal arrow running from M to P. Given full employment and a relatively stable velocity of money, any change in M must cause an *equiproportionate* change in P. Increase the money supply by 10 percent and prices will go up 10 percent. Inflation, consequently, is the result of increases in the money supply. To reduce inflation, reduce the money supply. It's as simple as all that. Real output, and hence employment, on the other hand is determined by productivity (investment) and thrift (savings) in the real sector of the economy, and flexible prices in competitive markets guarantee that the economic system will automatically hum along at full employment— provided that big unions, big business, and big government are somehow kept in check. There is, in other words, a dichotomy between the real and monetary sectors. One does not affect the other; the two are totally independent. The quantity theory of money is, therefore, a theory of the general price level, not of real output and employment.

All that remains is to allow for growth in real output over time. Full-employment output does not remain the same. The labor force grows over time as does the average productivity of labor both through increases in the skills of workers due to better education and living conditions and through the provision of the work force with increasingly sophisticated equipment (capital) with which to do its work. In such a world of a dynamically increasing full-employment real output, a constant money supply would become a drag on the economy. Relative to a growing full-employment Q, the fixed amount of money would slow down the real rate of growth and grind it eventually to a halt. Unemployment would then rise. In a growing economy, therefore, the money supply should not remain fixed if full employment is to be dynamically maintained. It, too, must grow in an accommodating way. But by how much? The answer is relatively simple and is critical for understanding neoclassical supply-side theory.

The quantity theory of money can be easily restated in growth terms using simple mathematics and ignoring cross products. $MV = PQ$ becomes

$$\dot{M} + \dot{V} = \dot{P} + \dot{Q}$$

where $\dot{M}$ is the relative rate of change or growth rate in the money supply, and similarly for $\dot{V}, \dot{P},$ and $\dot{Q}$. But if velocity is assumed to be stable, $\dot{V}$ is equal to zero and drops out of the equation, leaving us with:

$$\dot{M} = \dot{P} + \dot{Q}$$

which can be rewritten in terms of $\dot{P}$, or the rate of inflation:

$$\dot{P} = \dot{M} - \dot{Q}$$

If the growth rate in the money supply is greater than the growth rate in real output ($\dot{M} > \dot{Q}$), the price level will increase ($\dot{P} > 0$) by the amount of the difference. Therefore, to stop inflation dead in its track, all one has to do is to equate the growth rates of real output and the money supply. Clearly, if $\dot{M} = \dot{Q}$, then $\dot{P} = 0$ and the price level will be stable. It is a lovely, simple world to contemplate in all its shining splendor. It should be kept in mind, however, that $\dot{Q}$ is always a full-employment growth rate. It is also assumed that there is no trouble in identifying M or, for that matter, in measuring it.[1]

II

Keynesian theory, on the other hand, does not assume that real output will necessarily be at full employment. It admits the possibility of a stagnant economy at considerably less than full employment, as was amply demonstrated in the 1930s during the Great Depression. Real output and employment depend, in Keynesian theory, on the propensity of individuals to spend a certain proportion of their income on goods and services (consumption) and on the willingness of businessmen to invest in new plant and equipment (investment). The higher the level of real income, the higher the level of consumption. The relationship between consumption and income, however, is considered to be relatively stable in the absence of changes in the distribution of income and the tax schedules governing personal income. However, if taxes are reduced, disposable after-tax income will increase, leading to an increase in consumption expenditures and hence to an increase in total output and employment. As people in the aggregate consume more, more will be produced and employment will rise. But given the consumption-income relationship, and given the distribution of income and the underlying tax structure, real output and employment will depend primarily on the level of private investment and on the psychological profit expectations of businessmen. The profit expectations of businessmen, however, are taken to be highly volatile. When a chronic level of high unemployment exists, it is up to the government to stimulate aggregate demand by decreasing taxes on personal income (in order to increase consumption), or by decreasing business taxes (in order to induce an increase in investment by changing the profit expectation of businessmen), or by increasing government expenditures (in order to increase the amount of purchasing power in the economy)—or by some combination of all three. At the same time, tax cuts and increases in government expenditures generate budgetary deficits. Deficit financing to increase output and reduce the level of unemployment represents a Keynesian fiscal-policy approach to the problem of chronic unemployment.

Investment, which is the key variable in Keynesian economics, is also affected by the level of interest rates. A fall in interest rates will make formerly unprofitable or marginal investment projects profitable. Capital formation will take place and output and employment will increase by some multiple of the increase in investment as its effects ripple through the economy. There is, nonetheless, considerable dispute among Keynesians over the sensitivity of investment to interest-rate changes. Those who doubt that lower interest rates will have enough of an impact on investment to move the economy to full employment stress the need to change profit expectations either through cuts in business and personal income taxes or by increases in government expenditures. The same argument applies, though with somewhat lesser force, against increases in the rate of interest as a means for controlling inflation, or a state of over-full employment.

Changes in the level of interest rates are a matter of monetary policy, and in traditional Keynesian theory monetary policy plays a subordinate and supporting role in relation to fiscal policy. In Keynesian monetary theory, the total money supply is held, first, for transactions purposes, that is, to finance the imperfect synchronization of disbursements and receipts of households and such ongoing business requirements as the meeting of payrolls and the buying of raw materials needed in the production process, and to protect both households and businesses against unforeseen contingencies. It is also held for speculative purposes in the form of idle balances. Where transactions money is related primarily to the level of economic activity, speculative balances are seen to depend on the prevailing level of interest rates and the expectations concerning their future course. In the simplest of terms, the alternative cost of holding speculative cash balances at high interest rate levels (the interest income foregone in the act of holding cash) decreases the demand for cash balances and "activates" idle balances by decreasing their supply. At high interest rate levels, speculative cash balances are converted primarily into business transactions balances through the intermediation of the financial system. Although interest rate levels follow from the interaction of the demand and supply of money, the supply of money can be affected by actions of the central bank (the Federal Reserve System). When the money supply is restricted and the availability of credit declines, interest rates will rise. But the rise in interest rates will, in turn, cause idle balances to fall as they are converted into transactions balances. And a fall in idle balances, in Keynesian theory, is simply another way of talking about an increase in the income velocity of money.

Although Keynesians are not in complete agreement over the response of investment to changes in the interest rate (i), they are in complete agreement on the positive relationship between velocity and the rate of interest. In Keynes the $MV=PQ$ or $Y=MV$ equation becomes:

$$Y = M \bullet V(i)$$

where $V(i)$ means that velocity, contrary to the orthodox quantity theory of money, is not a constant. It responds directly to changes in the interest rate. An increase in the rate of interest *causes* an increase in the income velocity of money.

Velocity increases can take place for any of three reasons: (1) an activation of idle or speculative balances; (2) an economizing of transactions balances at very high interest rate levels; or (3) massive innovations in financial institutions such as NOW accounts, mutual funds, "sweep" accounts, certificates of deposit, the development of a Eurodollar market, and so on —all of which, along with (1) and (2), tend to offset and neutralize the attempts of the monetary authorities to restrict the money supply. There is, in short, not only an inverse relationship between interest rates and the money supply, but also an accompanying inverse relationship between interest rates and the income velocity of money.

Even if the economy were in the grip of inflation and $\dot{M}$ were set at less than $\dot{Q}$, prices could continue to rise for a while as a result of the rise in the velocity of money. The Keynesian variation on the quantity equation becomes:

$$\dot{P} = (\dot{M} - \dot{Q}) + \dot{V}$$

Reducing $\dot{M}$, or the growth rate of the money supply, below $\dot{Q}$ (or setting the two equal) does not guarantee a fall in $\dot{P}$ so long as $\dot{V}$ remains positive. That is, tight money and continuing inflation, in the immediate short run, are *not* mutually exclusive.

There is, however, a limit to velocity increases. In the face of a restricted money supply, they cannot go on forever. Eventually, all idle balances will be activated and the economizing of transactions balances will reach their outer limit. Financial innovations, on the other hand, take time to be set in place. A persistent restriction of the money supply will, in short order, cause real output to fall via the interest-rate effect on investment and by the dimmed profit expectations of businessmen which diminished credit availability will bring about. Within this set of circumstances, the relationship between prices, output, and money growth becomes $\dot{Q} = \dot{M} - \dot{P}$, and so long as $\dot{M}$ is low and $\dot{P}$ remains high, real output will fall and unemployment will rise.

But what of the effect of changes in the money supply on prices and the problem of inflation in general? Here orthodox Keynesians have not done too well. They have put a lot of faith in the Phillips curve—a curve purporting to show that the rate of inflation depends on the rate of unemployment and that a trade-off exists between the two. At low levels of unemployment and a general shortage of labor, unions are able to increase wages above the normal productivity increases of labor, with inflation as the result. With increasing taxes and lessening government expenditures, real output declines and the redundancy of labor, as unemployment rises, holds wages in line by undermining the power of unions, thus reducing the rate of inflation. Alternatively, by the use of persistent tight money, when velocity increases have been wrung out of the economy, the central bank can cause investment and hence output to decline in response to higher interest rates and their effect on investment. With $\dot{V}=0$ and $\dot{M}$ low, causing a fall in output and a rise in unemployment, we are squarely in the lap of the Phillips curve trade-off of Keynesian theory.

In traditional Keynesian economics, therefore, M and Q are not independent of each other. The neoclassical dichotomy does not apply. Changes in the monetary sector have, potentially, grave consequences for the real sector of the economy. With $\dot{V}>0$ serving as the immediate offset to $\dot{M}<\dot{Q}$, $\dot{Q}$ continues apace and the rate of inflation rises. In due course, when changes in the velocity of money grind to a halt, $\dot{M}<\dot{Q}$ causes real output to fall, which in turn causes $\dot{P}$ to fall via the unemployment-rate effect of the Phillips curve. Or, to state the matter another way: initially M and Q appear not to be related—giving the offhand impression that the classical dichotomy applies although, contrary to the quantity theory of money, P does not respond to a fall in $\dot{M}$. The price level continues to increase because of the short-term increases in the velocity of income, which has responded positively to the rise in the interest rate, itself the result of the fall in the money supply. Soon after, however, when velocity is at its maximum and ceases to increase, $\dot{M}$ and $\dot{Q}$ become positively related with a fall in $\dot{M}$ *causing* a fall in $\dot{Q}$ and $\dot{P}$, the latter via the Phillips curve trade-off.

In summary, interest rates have a critical role to play in Keynesian monetary theory. They are inversely related to money supply changes—which, as we shall see, the monetarist supply-side school flatly denies. In traditional Keynesian economics, contrary to the teachings of the quantity theory of money, *the money supply has no direct effect on the price level; its principal effect is on real output and the rate of unemployment.* The price level, in other words, is directly related only to the unemployment rate, and money-supply changes affect the price level indirectly through changes induced in the level of real output and employment.

But then something went wrong in the 1970s. High levels of

unemployment (low levels of real output) were now associated with increasing prices. The Phillips curve trade-off had broken down and Keynesian economics was caught in the bind of stagflation. If unemployment were high, fiscal policy should move the budget into deficit by lowering taxes and raising government expenditures. The government should also increase the money supply in the hope of increasing investment by bringing interest rates down. But if, *at the same time,* the rate of inflation were too high it should move toward a budgetary surplus by raising taxes and lowering government expenditures while tightening up the money supply in order to bring down private investment through higher interest rates. Keynesian policy was thus put into an impossible situation by being required to move in exactly opposite directions at one and the same time.

III

With orthodox Keynesians trapped in the quagmires of stagflation, the ground was prepared for the rise of supply-side economics. There has developed on the periphery, however, a new school of Post Keynesian economics. The Phillips curve is rejected outright and in its place a new theory of inflation is formulated that does not relate price-level changes to the unemployment rate. Nor does it accept the traditional view that prices depend on the money supply. The onus for inflation is put on the money wage rate directly. Labor markets are not competitive; money wages are *not* the result of the interplay of demand and supply. Wages, in other words, are not endogenous to the system. They are exogenously determined by collective bargaining. Nor, for that matter are the prices of goods determined by demand and supply in competitive goods markets. The economy is characterized by oligopolistic concentrations of market power with oligopolies setting their prices at some markup over unit wage costs—the markup being determined by the varying degrees of monopoly in different industries. If such is indeed the case, then

$$P = k\left(\frac{w}{A}\right)$$

where P is the price level, k is the degree of monopoly, w is the nominal or money wage rate, and A is the average productivity of labor. If k and A are relatively constant, then prices are causally related to the wage rate. To control the level of prices, the nominal wage rate must be controlled—not the money supply as in the quantity theory of money, or the rate of unemployment as in the Phillips curve approach of traditional Keynesians. To control inflation, according to the Post Keynesians, what is needed is an *incomes policy*. Specifically, the incomes policy most Post Keynesians prefer is a tax-based incomes policy (TIP) which increases the resistance of business to the wage demands of labor by penalizing those businesses which do not limit the wage rates they grant to the guidelines set down by the government. The penalty is linked to the corporate income tax. Assume the corporate income tax is 46 percent and the wage guideline of the government is 5 percent. If a corporation should grant a 10 percent increase in wages, a penalty of three times the difference could be added to the corporation's income tax; that is, the corporation would be required to pay $46\% + 3(5\%) = 61\%$ of its corporate profits. The corporation's tax liability becomes larger the more the negotiated wage rate exceeds the government's guideline. The merits, demerits, or even political feasibility of TIP aside, Post Keynesians are firmly convinced that prices depend on wage levels and, if inflation is to be controlled, so must wages be—until the wage rate can be brought gradually back in line with increases in the productivity of labor, at which point prices would be stable and the problem of inflation solved.

With an incomes policy based on the wage-price equation, $P = k(w/A)$, tight money and high interest rates would *not* be necessary; indeed, they would be counterproductive if not downright perverse. With the price level, or the rate of inflation, controlled by TIP, an easy-money policy could be followed without fear of increased prices. The lower interest rates would serve as a stimulus to investment through the interest-rate effect, however limited. Monetary policy would thus support the more powerful fiscal policies needed to increase output and employment. Post Keynesian economics, in other words, rejects the need to deflate the economy in order to bring down the price level via the higher unemployment rates of the Phillips curve, or excessive reductions in the money supply, which come out to the same thing in a Keynesian context.

Post Keynesian theory also rejects the quantity theory of money as do the orthodox Keynesians, but it does so by reversing the causal arrow between the money supply and the price level. In both the quantity theory of money and traditional Keynesian theory, the money supply is *exogenous*. It is determined by the Federal Reserve serving as the central bank of the U.S. economy. In Post Keynesian theory, the money supply is *endogenous*. It is passively accommodating to the needs of the economy. If so, then even orthodox Keynesian monetary policy is an exercise in futility. In Post Keynesian theory, financial innovations serve to undermine and offset the monetary constraints of the central bank. The fundamental relationship is:

$$\dot{M} \xleftarrow{} f(\dot{P})$$

with the causal arrow flowing from changes in the price level to the money supply: inflation is accommodated by changes in the money supply, in many cases beyond the reach of the monetary authorities. For Post Keynesians, there are no known limits to changes in the income velocity of money.

Banks are in business for profit, as are nonfinancial enterprises. They have customers who make up the major part of their earning assets (loans). In the 1950s, no matter what pressure the central bank put on their reserves, banks were able to replenish them by dumping their wartime-accumulated holdings of Treasury bills (TBs) rather than cutting back on their loans. As inflation continues and the need for money increases accordingly, banks will do what they can to accommodate the needs of their customers.

When the volume of bank-held TBs diminished by the 1960s, banks initiated negotiable certificates of deposit at high interest rates which caused deposits to shift from thrift institutions into commercial bank time deposits and from internally held high-reserve demand deposits to low-reserve time deposits (CDs), thereby increasing bank reserves and the lending power of the commercial banking system. The Eurodollar market was also quick to develop, which allowed banks to increase their lending ability outside the reserve requirements of the central bank. In the 1970s and early 1980s, apart from NOW accounts in both commercial and saving banks, against which checks can be written, other important developments have taken place outside the banking system and thus beyond the control of the monetary authorities. Examples are: corporate overnight repurchase agreements with banks (RPs), money market mutual funds, business "sweep" accounts which provide for automatic transfers between checking deposits and interest-paying investment accounts, floating bank rate notes combining long-term maturity with semiannual redemption privileges after a two-year waiting period, bank loan sales, documentary discount notes backed by banks, overdraft accounts, new cash management techniques, and so on and on and on.

The central bank has not only lost control over the monetary aggregates it seeks to control; it is also unable to define what "money" is, let alone measure and control it. Monetary policy has become a shambles. Velocity apparently knows no bounds.

In Post Keynesian theory, at any rate, inflation can occur regardless of the rate of unemployment. Even at high unemployment rates inflation will continue as long as wages increase by more than the productivity of labor and as long as businesses follow a markup pricing policy that allows them to pass the wage increases onto consumers by increasing their prices. Stagflation in this context is not a mystery. And monetary policy, whether of the traditional Keynesian or quantity theory type, either is not effective or is based on a false premise concerning the relationship of an exogenous money supply to the price level. Orthodox Keynesians and neoclassical monetarists both lack a key element: an effective *incomes policy*. Without it, inflation cannot be controlled except by wrecking the economy. It is very much like trying to stop a bleeding nose by applying a tourniquet around one's neck.

IV

We come finally to the modern quantity theory of money as it has been developed by Milton Friedman. It has been left for last since it forms the basis for the monetarist version of supply-side economics. Again, a highly simplified version will be given.

The "new" quantity theory of money is a variation on a Keynesian theme and therefore as much a demand-side theory as Keynesian theory is—a point which has not passed by George Gilder unnoticed. The restatement of the quantity theory begins with the proposition that the *nominal* gross national product (Y) is the product of a stable velocity function and the quantity of money, i.e.,

$$Y = V(\ ) \cdot M$$

where $V(\ )$ is the velocity function. It stipulates that velocity depends on a constellation largely of long-term interest rates representing the cost of holding money, the growth rate of the price level, the level of real income, some measure of wealth, and the asset preferences of individuals—all of which are included within the parentheses of $V(\ )$. In Friedman, however, the desire to hold money is not, as in Keynes, dependent on interest rates. The demand for money depends on real income per capita. Moreover, as real income increases, the demand for money increases more than proportionally—by almost double according to Friedman. Since velocity is the ratio of income to the money supply ($V = Y/M$), it follows that over the long run velocity will decline as a result of the more than proportionate increase in the demand for money in response to increases in the level of real income. That velocity has shown a marked tendency to rise in the postwar period in response to sharp increases in interest rates is a problem that Friedman has not been able to cope with successfully.

At any rate, in Friedmanian theory velocity is not influenced by interest rates. For all intents and purposes, the velocity *function* can be regarded as relatively stable. This is not the same as saying, as in the orthodox quantity theory, that velocity is a numerical constant. It does change, but it does so in a stable and predictable fashion in response to secular changes in real income per capita. Nominal income is therefore "determined" by changes in the quantity of money, however defined. That is,

$$Y = \overleftarrow{PQ = f(M)}$$

The causal arrow now runs not from M to P, as in the older quantity version, but from M to Y. In this sense, the older equiproportionality requirement does not hold. An increase in the money supply may well cause prices to increase, but not necessarily in the same proportion. Some will spill over into increases in real output—unless, of course, the economy is already at full employment. In that case changes in the price level are uniquely the result of changes in the money supply, and we are firmly situated in the original version of the quantity theory of money.

Friedman, however, believes that if free markets were allowed to prevail there would be a natural tendency toward full employment *in the long run*. In the long run, therefore, the price level would be stable if the growth rate in the money supply were equated to the long-run natural or full employment growth path of the economy. That is, if $\dot{M} = \dot{Q}$, then $\dot{P} = 0$ and the problem of inflation would be solved—at least in the long run.

The interest rates of Keynesian theory are irrelevant and so is the wage rate that is so critical to Post Keynesian theory. If we followed Friedman's monetary rule of setting $\dot{M}$ equal to $\dot{Q}$, all would be in order. Short-run problems should not sway us from following this rule, and the Federal Reserve should be reduced to a strictly check-clearing operation. The Federal Reserve cannot be trusted to exercise any discretionary judgment because its attempts to manipulate the money supply contracyclically are bound to be perverse since so little is known, or can be known on any reliable basis, of the time lags involved in the exercise of monetary restraint or ease. That is, since we cannot know with any assurance, at any particular time, where exactly we are on the business cycle, and since we cannot know the time it will take for various monetary policies to affect the economy, it is best not to try to apply human intelligence to the solution of social problems. In our ignorance of the world and the way it works, we should rely solely on a mechanical rule and do nothing on a discretionary basis.

There is an act of faith involved here. It is the deep belief that the quantity theory of money is true, that in fact the price level in the long run is exclusively dependent on the money supply. If, on the other hand, it is not, then Friedman's policy prescriptions turn out to be pernicious in that not only will suffering be ignored in the short-run; it will not be alleviated in the long run either. Throughout the ages chiliastic prophets have always believed that the pains of today are the price that must be paid for the deliverance of tomorrow. An awful lot is riding on the quantity theory of money as catechism. It is a catechism that ignores the short-run concerns of Keynesians and worships at the altar of the long run.

Implicit in Friedman's monetarism are several secondary propositions that follow from his version of the quantity theory of money. One is the "crowding-out thesis," which argues that Keynesian fiscal policy has no effect on the real sector of the economy, that tax cuts and increases in government expenditures cannot affect the level of real output or the rate of unemployment. Their only impact is on the composition and level of *nominal* income—a remarkable proposition at face value which will be featured prominently in neoclassical supply-side theory.

The crowding-out hypothesis argues that the use of Keynesian fiscal policy to fight unemployment requires a cut in taxes, or an increase in government expenditures, or both. The resulting deficit will have to be financed by borrowing from the public. What government pumps into the economy on the one hand, it will take out with the other, leaving total spending in the economy unchanged. The financing of the deficit by the Treasury's sale of government securities will cause an excess supply of bonds, which will force their price down. A fall in bond prices, however, implies an increase in interest rates. Since investment, to monetarists, is highly sensitive to the level of interest rates (unlike the traditional Keynesian belief) private investment will decline by an amount equal to the deficit—thereby offsetting the stimulus of the government's fiscal policy. Nominal GNP will therefore not change since the increase in government expenditures, for example, merely displaces the decrease in private expenditures, and fiscal policy turns out to be irrelevant. The same applies for a tax cut.

The crowding-out thesis, however, depends on three very critical assumptions: (1) that the demand for money is independent of the rate of interest, which is another way of saying that the velocity of money function is stable; (2) that investment is highly sensitive to the rate of interest, which means that even a small increase in interest rates (because of government bond sales) will yield a disproportionate decline in private investment spending as an offset to government spending; and, perhaps most important of all, (3) that *the money supply is kept constant,* that is, the government deficit is not "monetized."

If, however, velocity responds to changes in the interest rate, and if investment is less sensitive to interest rates than monetarists maintain, the crowding-out hypothesis does not hold—at least not to the extent required—and real output and the rate of unemployment will respond to the government's fiscal-policy initiatives. Most critical to the crowding-out thesis is the assumption that the money supply is fixed. Since an increase in velocity represents an *indirect* increase in the money supply, the assumption that the demand for money is totally interest-insensitive is critical. But even beyond that convenient assumption, it is difficult to see why a Keynesian government would not allow an appropriate increase in support of its antiunemployment fiscal policy, particularly for an economy operating at considerably below capacity. The monetarist answer is simple: an increase in the money supply would have an inflationary impact on the price level, which is, of course, anathema. Again, a sensible response is ruled out because of an abiding *belief* in a highly dubious theory of inflation. It is also apparent that the discrediting of Keynesian fiscal policy is a theoretical ploy. Monetarists start with some version of the quantity theory of money as an article of faith and march resolutely backward making whatever assumptions are necessary, along the way, to get them to where they want to go.

Another corollary of monetarist economics is the metaphysical notion of a "natural" unemployment rate. Key to the theory of a natural unemployment rate is the assumption that the labor market is competitive with the real wage rate set by the demand and supply of labor. Involuntary unemployment cannot exist in such a market; unemployment is either voluntary or frictional. When the labor market is cleared, all those willing to work at the market-determined real wage are able to do so. In such an equilibrium, according to Friedman, the *actual* rate of inflation will be equal to the *expected* rate and prices will not change. Assume we are at the natural unemployment rate (whatever that is)[2] with a zero rate of inflation but that do-good Keynesians find the unemployment rate intolerable. Accordingly, they initiate the needed fiscal and monetary policies to lower the short-term unemployment rate to that level they find socially desirable. According to the Phillips curve trade-off, prices will rise forcing real wages down. At the lower level of real wages, an excess demand for labor will exist in the competitive labor market. The system will have become destabilized. Money wages will be bid up as a result until the initial equilibrium real wage rate is restored at the "natural" unemployment rate.

In the long run, therefore, Keynesian fiscal policy has no permanent effect on the unemployment rate and has only succeeded in raising the price level by its self-defeating actions. The argument is much more complicated than this, but the argument presented does give a fairly accurate picture of the monetarist notion of the "natural" unemployment rate and the futility of Keynesian monetary and fiscal policies in trying to alter this long-run, natural state of affairs. Since the Keynesian mix of fiscal and monetary policy can have no lasting effect on the rate of unemployment—it can only result in higher price levels at the long-run, natural rate of unemployment—it would be better to keep the government budget balanced at all times and use monetary policy to stabilize the price level by following Friedman's monetary rule. Along with the crowding-out hypothesis, the notion of the natural rate of unemployment drives home a second nail in Keynes's coffin.

There is a third. The nominal interest rate is not determined by the demand and supply for money, even though almost everything else is. The nominal interest rate looks forward to the course of future events. And in these future events the *expected* rate of inflation is paramount. The nominal interest rate—the one actually observed—consists of the sum of the expected real rate of interest (determined in the real sector by productivity and thrift) and the expected rate of inflation. According to the Federal Reserve Bank of St. Louis, a bastion of monetarism, the real rate of interest has been relatively stable in the postwar period at about 2 or 3 percent. Changes in the nominal interest rate must therefore be attributable to expected changes in the price level, i.e.,

$$i = f(\dot{P})$$

If, in the short run, a Keynesian easy-money policy causes the nominal interest rate to fall, such a fall will be quickly reversed as the increase in the money supply causes prices to rise, which, in turn, will cause the nominal interest rate to rise and more than overtake the initial, short-run fall. We could add "in the long run" but in this case the long run is not all that long—the effect will be quickly realized, according to the monetarists. If the nominal interest rate is an inflationary markup over the real rate of interest, and the rate of inflation depends on the money supply growth rate, then it follows that the nominal interest rate depends exclusively on the rate of growth of the money supply. Put more directly:

If $i = f(\dot{P})$, and $\dot{P} = f(\dot{M})$, then $i = f(\dot{M})$, all positively related.

What we wind up with is the very un-Keynesian proposition that *easy money causes interest rates to rise and tight money causes them to fall*—a startling proposition, to say the least.

The quantity theory of money, as developed by the monetarists, yields a very comforting thought. If we keep the growth rate of the money supply equal to the natural growth rate of the economy: (1) the problem of inflation will be solved; (2) interest rates will be lower than they would otherwise be; (3) the economy will be at its natural, minimum feasible unemployment rate; and (4) it will be at a permanent full-employment output level—if only we could do something about the problem of big unions and big business, the interferences of big government, and the meddling of misguided Keynesians.

It is a comfortable, if somewhat simpleminded, view of *The Way the World Works*—to use Jude Wanniski's presumptuous book title. All you have to do is follow a mechanical monetary rule and everything will fall neatly into place, without any need to strain the limited resources of discretionary human intelligence. As a burlesque queen was once overheard to say, "If you wanna make a success of it, you gotta have a gimmick." In the case of the monetarists, the gimmick is the money supply. They have used it to strip the real world of all its complexity.

It is this simpleminded monetarist *weltanschauung* that two key epigones of Milton Friedman, currently serving as Under Secretaries of the Treasury, have wedded to supply-side economics, and it is to their teachings that we now turn.

Notes

[1]This will turn out to be extremely difficult, as we shall see—as will maintaining the presumed stability of V, not to mention Q bobbing merrily along its full-employment path.

[2]In Friedman's own words (1968): "Unfortunately, we have as yet devised no method to estimate accurately or readily the natural rate of interest or unemployment."

CHAPTER 4

Monetarist Supply-Side Economics

I

In earlier times, before the 1930s collapse, it was assumed that market forces would keep the economy at its natural full-employment level, at least over the long run. Short-run deviations were temporary and automatically corrected, without any need for government intervention. Indeed, government intervention, along with such market imperfections as big business and big unions, would serve only to thwart the natural tendency of the system toward the most efficient allocation of resources. The optimum level of income, in an ideal market system, was taken as given, short-run wiggles aside.

In such a world, attention is focused, almost exclusively, on relative prices and their quick response to changes in the personal preferences of all *individuals* comprising the economy. Changes in relative prices in a smoothly functioning market system therefore determine the allocation of scarce resources and guarantee maximum efficiency with output at full employment. Price effects are all; income effects are irrelevant.

Prices, of course, were seen to be determined in competitive factor markets governing labor and capital as well as in competitive goods markets. The *distribution* of the given total output is therefore determined by relative factor prices and their "marginal productivity," or their successive contributions to total output. In this neoclassical system it is *assumed* that classes do not exist— only individuals seeking, in total indifference to the welfare of others, to maximize their own individual well-being. There is, in other words, no class struggle over the division of the spoils. The rule of distribution is simple: *From each according to his ability, to each according to his contribution*—with the corollary: you don't work, you don't eat! Claims on the social product are to be restricted to those who, by the sweat of their brow, help produce the output that is to be distributed by impersonal market forces. Because people have different talents and abilities, so are their rewards different—provided they choose to put them to social use. As Herbert Spencer unflinchingly put it, "The command 'if any could not work neither should he eat' is simply a Christian enunciation of that universal law of nature under which life has reached its present height—the law that a creature not energetic enough to maintain itself must die."

Under the market's rule for distribution it follows that the division of the social product among productive individuals of different talents and abilities cannot be equal. It is not a matter of counting noses and dividing that sum into the total social output. Of necessity, the distribution has to be unequal if the maximum social happiness is to be attained. But it is "just." You get according to what you give. What could be fairer than that? And if, for any reason, you cannot give, so you have no claim to life. Economic euthanasia leaves no room for the transfer payments of bleeding-heart liberal intellectuals. Just as you cannot tamper with the laws of God or Nature, without bringing retribution down upon your head, so you cannot tamper with the laws of economics. Seeming cruelty is the greatest kindness of all, for it guarantees the greatest happiness of the greatest number. And it leaves no place for freeloaders or social parasites who, though able, choose to lead the idle life. What they need most is the spur, not the handout.

It also follows that the greater reward's going to the more talented and the more able gives the system a dynamic edge. Interfere with this "natural" distribution of the market system and you undermine the work efforts of those who have the most to contribute. With the incentives of the more productive classes dulled, they opt for more leisure; and, with less work from those most able to provide it, the social output must necessarily decline and the level of social misery increase. This last is, of course, the favorite litany of classical supply-siders, such as George Gilder and Jude Wanniski—two popular journalists with little formal training in economics. Monetary supply-siders, though subscribing to the main incentive tenets of Gilder and Wanniski—with, as we shall see, the exception of the Laffer curve—are theoretically more sophisticated. They are generally Chicago economists who seek to combine supply-side theory with the monetarist theories of Milton Friedman—a combination that threatens to blow apart the whole of supply-side economics. The two main protagonists of the monetarist version of supply-side economics are Norman Ture and Beryl Sprinkel. We shall look at the arguments of each in turn.

II

Norman Ture, before his appointment as Under Secretary of Tax and Economic Policy of the U.S. Treasury Department in the Reagan Administration,[1] was president of the ultraconservative Institute for Research on the Economics of Taxation (IRET) and an adjunct scholar of the equally conservative American Enterprise Institute for Policy Research, both based in Washington, D.C. He studied at the University of Chicago where he received his Ph.D. in economics in 1968, at the age of 44, and on the side in addition to his other activities ran the economic consulting firm of Norman B. Ture, Inc., also located in Washington.

It was as president of IRET that he delivered a paper (November 12, 1980) outlining his version of supply-side economics to the Economic Round Table of the Lehrman Institute.[2]

Whereas classical supply-siders emphasize their classical roots, Ture attributes the conceptual origin of supply-side economics to "the neoclassical theoretical traditions." He agrees with the classical supply-side school that government spending should be curtailed and that tax cuts are needed to stimulate work incentives and increase savings, the latter leading to an automatic increase in capital formation. Although he favors the monetarist prescription for "slowing the rate of increase in the stock of money"—an argument that Beryl Sprinkel, as we shall see, pursues with the maniacal fervor of a true believer—his basic theoretical approach is the microeconomics of neoclassical price theory. For Ture, " 'Supply-side' economics is merely the application of price theory . . . to economic aggregates" (p. 4), and "its conceptual antecedents are to be found in the work of the classical economists of the modern era . . . —from Adam Smith through Milton Friedman and Gary Becker" (p. 5).[3]

Monetarist, or neoclassical supply-siders, believe in the inherent stability of the market system, if not tampered with. Resources, via competitive and therefore flexible prices, will be optimally allocated leading the economy toward its inherent long-run, full-employment potential—or, in what amounts to the same thing, to its lowest *feasible* unemployment rate (Friedman's "natural" rate of unemployment). Post Keynesians, on the other hand, face up to the existence of oligopolistic price rigidities and money illusion (that people do not think exclusively in real terms). Above all, they recognize that *uncertainty* about the future permeates all economic decisions. For them, in particular, uncertainty does not imply ignorance of an immutable noumenal world which is knowable in principle. Uncertainty is inherent in the economic system whose underlying structure is in a constant state of flux. It is the difference between uncertainty in a neoclassical Newtonian universe and the profound and insoluble uncertainty to be found in quantum theory—where the subject-object relationship cannot be separated. The very act of observation changes the nature of what is being observed. Similarly, in the social sciences, "facts" take on relevance only within a theoretical context and cannot be separated from values. At any rate, the Post Keynesian notion of uncertainty leaves no room for the neoclassical idea of "equilibrium." But even in conventional Keynesian theory, which does rely on equilibrium analysis, the economy does not tend automatically toward a full-employment equilibrium. Indeed, the economy could well get stuck at a depressed level with a chronic rate of severe unemployment. All this is brushed aside by supply-siders of the monetarist stripe.

For Ture and his followers relative prices are paramount. And it is the effect of government actions on relative prices that requires the closest theoretical scrutiny. The economy is broken down into two sectors: the government sector and the private sector, the latter consisting of individual households (consumers) and businesses (producers). The first-order effect of government spending and taxing is on relative prices—they are altered. The private sector then responds to these government-induced changes in relative prices by reallocating resources accordingly. The second-order private response to government activity, which takes place "more or less promptly," affects the *composition* of total output. Whether it affects the real level of economic activity or only its nominal value depends on the nature of government activity. If aggregate demand is initially given, then the *right kind* of government activity may cause relative prices to change in such a redistributive way that real output and employment increase. "The distributional consequences of fiscal action," then, are critical.

The fact is that, for most supply-siders, government fiscal policies in the past have *not* played such a positive role. "The basic 'supply-side' proposition," writes Ture, "*denies* the possibility that government action can *initially* and *directly* change the total real income of the economy" (p. 6, italics supplied). Insofar as government actions affect real output and hence the level of employment, such actions are secondary and indirect. However that may be, supply-siders flatly deny that Keynesian fiscal policy can have any effect on real output and employment. Tax cuts may increase disposable income, but such increases will not, of themselves, cause aggregate demand to increase. Hence Keynesian fiscal policy, for reasons to be made clear in a moment, will have no positive effect on real output and employment. Indeed deficits induced by contracyclical tax cuts and increases in government expenditures will serve to increase only the *nominal* value of a given real output via price increases, the latter being brought about by monetization of the public debt.

If so, then what does cause changes in real output? How can real output increase? The answer, in supply-side terms, is relatively easy. It is changes in real output that cause changes in real aggregate demand, not the other way round. It is, in other words, the supply side that dominates; demand merely follows in the wake of supply. But then what causes a change in supply? The answer is: a change in inputs. The next question is obvious. If changes in output can occur only as a result of changes in input, then what causes a change in input? The answer is equally simple: a change in incentives. Let's start with the changes in output.

"Changes in output [real income]," writes Ture, "occur only as a result of changes in the amount of production inputs or the intensity or efficiency of their use." He goes on: "To have a first-order effect on income . . . government actions would have to alter directly the amount or effectiveness of production units committed to production" (p. 7). So far, so good; it seems sensible. The key is that government actions should be of the right kind; that is, those government actions which increase the commitment of inputs to production. Government does, after all, have a role to play in increasing the level of real output and employment, but, unlike Keynesian prescriptions, it works indirectly by inducing the appropriate changes in the attitudes and motivations of those who supply the inputs—workers and businessmen. An increase "in the amount of production units committed to production will result only if the real rewards for their use, i.e., the real price received per unit of input, is changed" (p. 7). This requires some explanation. It is the "incentive" argument of classical supply-side economics with a bit more "theoretical" flair. The simpleminded Mary S. arguments of Jude Wanniski have no place here.

All taxes have what Ture calls an "excise effect"—they affect relative prices and costs. What we have to separate here is the effect of taxes on relative prices from their effect on work effort. All taxes affect relative prices, but regressive excise and sales taxes have virtually no effect on work effort—only progressive personal income taxes do. And since leisure is not taxed, income taxes raise the cost of work relative to leisure. In other words, although all government taxes distort the allocation of resources in the economy through their effect on relative prices, only the progressive tax on individual incomes affects the willingness of people to allocate their time between work and leisure. Regressive taxes may affect the *composition* of aggregate real output, but only income taxes can have a pronounced effect on the *level* of real output and employment.

The incentive, or work-effect, model of taxation is simple in its complexity. Work is onerous. Given a choice people would rather not. In paradise, where all goods are in infinitely elastic supply at zero price (you can have as much as you want for free), all 24 hours of each day would be allocated to leisure and none to work. It would be a delicious polymorphously perverse world. But ours is a world of scarcity, which puts a price on everything, and one needs to work in order to eat, pay the rent, educate oneself and one's children, and so on. There are no free lunches. You've got to work, like it or not. You've got to give up some of your leisure. The question is, how much? Since there are only 24 hours to the day, each extra hour of work means giving up an extra hour of leisure. Next, assume you are free to determine how many hours you will work and how many you will devote to play. You then, at a given hourly wage rate, allocate your time between work and leisure such that you will, in this world of scarcity, maximize your level of happiness. Using Ture's model, assume the hourly wage rate is $10 per hour. For each additional hour of work you will get the flat rate of $10. But the *value* of each hour of leisure you have to give up for each additional hour of work will mount. In equilibrium, you stop at that point where the marginal cost of leisure will be equal to $10, with, say, 8 hours devoted to work, 8 to sleep, and 8 to play. It's the best you can do. Although you would be happier with 16 hours of leisure and 8 for sleep, 8-8-8 represents the most happiness you can squeeze out of a 24-hour day and still meet your needs.

Along comes the government, which slaps a 25 percent tax on your hourly wage. Your after-tax take-home pay falls to $7.50 an hour. Your wage rate is still $10 an hour but taking an extra hour of leisure will now cost you $7.50, not $10. Given your particular sensitivity to work, you now find that your happiness will be maximized by working only 6 hours a day and adding the extra two hours to your leisure time. Your maximum happiness profile is now 6-10-8. What do you do? You go into your boss and say, "Look, the government has just hit me with an income tax, so beginning tomorrow I'll be coming in to work at 11 in the morning instead of 9." And what does your boss say? "That's OK; they've done the same to me so I'll be cutting down my work hours as well." And so does everyone else at the factory by varying degrees, depending on the lay of their happiness functions. With everyone working less, real output will clearly decline. But note that unemployment will *not* increase. Though output will be less because of a fall in input, the fall in input is *voluntary* and the economy is therefore still at full employment. There is no involuntary unemployment since the competitive market system is in full swing. This is flirting with the absurd!

Turn the model around and what do we have? The famous supply-side argument that a cut in taxes will cause output to increase by causing people to work more—the increase in input that Ture found as the only source for an increase in real output. Though the natural unemployment *rate* will not have changed, the *level* of voluntary employment will be higher leading therefore to a higher level of real output. Whether or not the increase in output will cause tax revenues to increase on a net basis (the Laffer effect) is another matter to which we will turn later.

III

The next building block of this neoclassical version of supply-side economics is the so-called "crowding-out" effect—a mainstay of monetarist economics. It is the basis for denying any Keynesian fiscal policy effect on real output and employment, and on that score it should be looked at carefully and reexamined.

Assume a balanced budget, where government tax revenues are

exactly equal to government expenditures. For whatever reason, unemployment rises and the government follows a Keynesian policy of cutting taxes in order to stimulate an increase in real output and employment by increasing disposable, after-tax income. The Keynesian assumption is that a significant part of the increase in disposable income will be spent on consumer goods causing businessmen to employ more labor to meet the induced increase in aggregate demand. The government budget, at least initially, will be in deficit with the unchanged level of government expenditures now exceeding the amount of its tax revenues by the amount of the tax cut. Alternatively, the same deficit could be realized by holding taxes constant and raising government expenditures in the form of increased transfer payments to persons or increased purchases of goods and services.

For monetary supply-siders, the loss in tax revenue is exactly equal to the deficit incurred, and the need of the Treasury to finance the debt, at whatever interest rate it takes, will totally absorb the increase in disposable income leaving no room for an increase in the total amount of spending. It is the composition, not the level, of aggregate demand that is changed. Similarly an increase in transfer payments to those in need (e.g., extended unemployment compensation) means that others must reduce their spending in order to buy the new government securities, while an increase in government purchases will serve only to displace purchases in the private sector. "Taking account of the fact that the private sector must, at the outset, reduce its spending in an amount equal to the deficit, it is clear," to Ture, "that no increase in aggregate demand can, initially, result" (p. 8).

The "crowding-out" hypothesis is a theory of preemption, a zero-sum game. Government expenditures "preempt the production resources of the nation for purposes determined in the political forum," we are told, "rather than in the marketplace, thereby depriving the private sector of these resources, the output they would produce, and the income claims generated by the production of these outputs" (p. 16). Government expenditures, in short, are sterile in that they add nothing to the productive capacity of the economy. Except for the *right kind* of cuts in taxes and cuts in government expenditures, the government's fiscal actions will have no effect on the real sector of the economy. Transfer payments, on the other hand, do not serve as built-in stabilizers mitigating the fall in aggregate purchasing power. They are, in the supply-side perception of "reality," a negative tax on leisure which "reduces the cost of not working and raises the cost of employment" and serves only to trap the poor in the welfare system and the unemployed in their unemployment. They also inhibit wage renegotiations and prolong recessions by preventing wages from falling. Medicaid transfer payments increase the cost of medical services by their easy accessibility and overuse, and aid to dependent children reduces the cost of being unemployed and the cost of raising children. Such costs are not market-determined. (Raising the real cost of having children, presumably, would result in fewer children!) In short, well-intentioned but misguided transfer payments, according to Ture, "constrain the supplies of production inputs, particularly labor, . . . enhance the downward rigidity of wage rates, and . . . distort relative prices of subsidized services" (p. 18); i.e., the market-determination of relative prices is not allowed to operate resulting in a distorted and less than optimal allocation of real resources in the economy. If transfer payments were drastically reduced, people would be forced to work, leading to an increase in real output and a decrease in poverty. Transfer payments, therefore, do not alleviate poverty (the postwar record notwithstanding); they perpetuate it. George Gilder would agree.

Implicit in the "crowding-out" argument, however, is the assumption that the public debt is not "monetized," which is to say that the central bank does not increase the money supply in order to facilitate the Treasury's financing of the debt. This seems to be a convenient assumption for supply-siders. Without it, their entire argument would collapse—fiscal policy would have a direct effect on output and employment, not merely a moderate indirect effect, as we shall see, through the incentive effect. It is on the issue of the "crowding-out" hypothesis that monetarist, neoclassical supply-siders are to be distinguished from their more classical brethren.

Neoclassical supply-siders, though paying lip service to the classical version, are at bottom monetarists. And it is as monetarists that they oppose the monetization of the public debt.

If the central bank were to increase the money supply to accommodate an increase in the public debt, the private sector would not have to reduce its outlays in order to absorb the increased debt. In that event, according to the quantity theory of money, there would be "an increase in aggregate *nominal* demand" (p. 9, original italics) and the effect would therefore be exclusively on the price level. Indeed, the existence or nonexistence of a deficit is beside the point: "Monetary expansion, whether or not associated with an increase in the government's deficit . . ., must surely result in an increase in nominal aggregate demand. But this increase . . . can, in turn, result *only* in an increase in the price level" (p. 9, italics supplied). *We are smack in the hands of the quantity theory of money in its fullest and most traditional sense, for, if an increase in the money supply can have no effect on real output, then the price level must increase equiproportionately to the increase in the money supply.*

Moreover, unlike changes in government taxes and expenditures, an "increase in the money stock," according to Ture, "has no relative price effect" in the sense that it will *not* "reduce the cost of effort relative to leisure" (p. 9). Nor will the increased money supply affect the "cost of saving and investment relative to consumption." Its *sole* effect will be on the price level. It is at this point that things *seem* to get unstuck, for, unless tax rates are fully indexed, the rise in prices will push individuals up into higher income tax brackets, thereby increasing the real marginal tax rate. And with an inflation-induced rise in the marginal tax rate, work incentives will be affected leading to a decrease in inputs and thus to a decrease in the level of real output. The apparent contradiction is resolved by distinguishing between *relative* prices and the *general* price level. An increase in the money supply does not affect relative prices, according to Ture. It affects only the general price level. And it is only changes in relative prices that will have a negative effect on work incentives and the allocation of resources between saving-investment and consumption, leading to a fall in real output. And with a slowing down of the real rate of growth, the problem of inflation will become even more pronounced. On the other hand, with fully indexed tax rates, the quantity theory of money would reign without qualification: relative prices would remain unchanged and the proportionate increase in the general price level would have no negative effect on inputs—real output would be unaffected. We can now wait with bated breath for January 1, 1985, when tax rates will be fully indexed for inflation.

It should be apparent that the crowding-out thesis is entirely dependent on the quantity theory of money. Without it, the need to hold the money supply in check would disappear, and so would the crowding-out hypothesis. Keynesians do not subscribe to the quantity theory of money and Post Keynesians, in particular, employ a markup theory of pricing, based on the degree of monopoly and unit prime costs, to explain inflation. No self-respecting Keynesian would therefore advocate holding the money supply constant in the face of a high level of unemployment. Instead, monetary policy would act to support the deficit financing of the Treasury by increasing the money supply and bringing interest rates down. Moreover, the crowding-out effect is highly unlikely in an economy running at considerably less than full-capacity utilization. The private demand for credit would be minimal. Under such circumstances, Keynesian deficit financing could act as a spur to investment and hence to an increase in real output and employment.

The crowding-out hypothesis hangs on making the control of inflation—on the basis of a very dubious theory—a more important social priority than reducing unemployment. It is the monetarist's bugaboo about monetizing the public debt and their blind faith in the validity of the quantity theory of money that invalidates, for them, Keynesian attempts to deal with the economic problem of unemployment. It is not that monetary supply-siders have "disproved" the Keynesian theory of aggregate demand and the effectiveness of a fiscal-monetary policy mix. It is rather in the name of the quantity theory of money that they are determined not to allow it to work by holding the money supply constant. That is, they are willing to tolerate high levels of unemployment in the short run in the *belief* that a monetarist monetary policy will solve the problems of employment in the long run.

What are the policy prescriptions of Norman Ture's version of supply-side economics? (pp. 21-26, italics supplied):

> (1) There is no pay-off in focusing fiscal policy on the control of aggregate demand.
> (2) A policy focus on the total amount of tax revenues is inappropriate as a means of influencing the level or change in total economic activity.
> (3) The size of the deficit should not be perceived as a relevant variable for policy manipulation in the interests of attaining designated levels—or rates of growth—in employment output, income, etc.
> (4) Public economic policy should substantially forego short run economic stabilization as a policy objective and focus, instead, on more attainable and relevant concerns [i.e., holding down inflation].

And perhaps most important of all, considering the conviction of many conservatives that the budget deficits of the government are the primary cause of inflation:

> (5) *"Supply-side" analysis leads to the rejection of the view that budget deficits per se are inflationary or that increases in government outlays are the root cause of inflation.* The pseudoscientific view of budget deficits as a source of inflation rests on the observation that those deficits tend to be monetized. This is not an inherent or necessary consequence of budget deficits.

From this, it follows that

> (6) the traditional link between monetary expansion and government deficits should be broken. Monetary policy should pursue a firm policy of steady growth in the stock of money substantially oblivious to budget prospects and outcomes.

To drive the point home:

> (7) Growth in government spending, *even at very rapid rates,* is not properly seen as the cause of inflation. . . . The tie between growth in spending and inflation is to be found in an excessively accommodating monetary policy. . . . The root cause of inflation—increases in the overall level of prices—*always* has been too fast a growth in the stock of money relative to the growth in real output.

With these extended quotations it is clear that classical supply-side economics has been almost totally submerged, if not drowned, in monetarist theory—a distinction which, in the end, will lead to a parting of the ways between the classical and monetarist schools of supply-side economics. But before getting into this debate we turn now to the most unrepentant of all monetarists, Ture's colleague in the Treasury, Under Secretary for Monetary Affairs, Beryl Sprinkel.

IV

Beryl Sprinkel, like Ture, is a product of the University of Chicago where he received his Ph.D. degree in economics in 1952. He went to work immediately thereafter for the Harris Trust and Savings Bank in Chicago where he attained the level of Executive Vice President and Economist in 1974. He is by far one of the most inflexible monetarists to be found anywhere. He puts Milton Friedman to the pale.

In keeping with his doctrinaire monetarist convictions he rejects any notion of a long-run trade-off between inflation and the rate of unemployment. He is a firm advocate of the "natural" rate of unemployment, and he is in complete agreement with Ture that "there is no long term relation between money and real growth."[4] He is also a great believer in the "crowding-out" hypothesis:

> When the Federal government finances a deficit by selling debt securities, it adds to the demand for credit in the financial mar-

kets. A deficit, therefore, absorbs credit in the private financial markets. It transfers to the public sector financial resources from the private sector (Senate Budget Committee: October 20, 1981).

If the deficit is not monetized, the government "acquires money from purchasing securities and then returns the money to the public when it pays for the deficit expenditures." All we have is a shuffling around of the ownership of money; the total money supply is unchanged, and with the money supply unchanged deficits cannot have any impact on the price level. Ture was quite emphatic on this point. To attribute inflation to government spending, with the money supply constant, would be "pseudoscientific." Sprinkel does not quite agree: "The negative effects of government borrowing originate in the credit markets—crowding out private investment and restricting growth. . . . For a given rate of monetary expansion, less growth in the economy means more inflation. *In this sense budget deficits are inflationary.*" And with the slackening off of the economy, tax revenues will fall, adding further to the deficit. Classical supply-side theory can be brought in to explain the fall in output and a secondary rise in the deficit. The supply-side incentive tax cut is supposed to result in an *increase* in output, but with the money supply held constant (or growing only at the natural growth rate of the economy), the increase in savings due to the tax cut (assuming little, if any, spills over into consumption, since the tax cut favors the rich, who have a high propensity to save) will in large part be absorbed by the Treasury's financing of the deficit. Investment will not rise significantly, if at all, since investment depends exclusively on savings in supply-side theory, and output will also not rise, or will rise by less than classical supply-siders would lead us to expect. Tight money (with a nonmonetized deficit), which monetary supply-siders insist upon, therefore mitigates if it does not totally offset (depending on the size of the deficit to be financed) the output-incentive effect of classical supply-side fiscal policy. The two camps would seem to be working at cross-purposes. Sprinkel is not to be deterred. While a nonmonetized budget deficit "can add to long-term inflationary pressure [by inducing a fall in real output], its effect on inflation is *small* compared to that of excessive monetary growth" (italics supplied). That is, monetarism is to be preferred even if it tends to offset the output effects of a classical supply-side tax cut or cut in government expenditures. But if monetarism undercuts classical supply-side fiscal policy, what happens to the Laffer curve?

It is here that the classical and the monetarist version of supply-side theory part company, despite the claims of compatibility which, not surprisingly, come exclusively from the monetarist camp. Says Ture:

> The supply side and monetarist analytics are merely variations on a single price theoretic theme.
>
> ....
>
> Supply-siders and monetarists are in perfect accord that in the long run, monetary aggregates do not determine real output.

Echoes Sprinkel:

> Monetarism and supply-side economics are completely complementary.

No such statements can be found on the classical supply side. Indeed, George Gilder flatly rejects the contention—and for good reason (see Ch. 2, pp. 38-41 above). For classical supply-siders, taxes are the cause of inflation, not deficits and not the money supply! The parting of their company is not difficult to explain. It has to do with the Laffer curve. Monetarist supply-siders do not deny the incentive effects of a classical supply-side tax cut. It's just that they don't think the output response will be all that great, and, being relatively small, its contribution to solving the persistent problem of inflation will also be trivial and of secondary importance to controlling the money-supply growth rate. Ture is quite explicit in rejecting the Laffer curve:

> Enthusiasm for "supply-side" policy was sometimes inadequately constrained by careful reasoning; some proponents [e.g., Laffer, Wanniski, Gilder, and Kemp] were inclined to claim too much. One of these excessive claims is that "supply-side" tax reductions will so expand GNP as to generate larger tax revenues than will be realized without tax cuts. This sort of fiscal alchemy . . . has misdirected much of the discussion about "supply-side" economics (p. 4).

Ture's protégé, David C. Raboy, refers to the Laffer curve as "a fiscal free lunch." He does not deny that output will expand as a result of a supply-side tax cut. More revenue will be generated by virtue of the increase in real output, but by no means as much as to offset the initial fall in revenues due to the tax cut itself. Ture, himself, is brutal in his dismissal of the Laffer curve.[5]

> I have never seen an Arthur Laffer model that was operational. It is all a set of equations put together. In my shop [IRET] we tried to use it and couldn't. I am not trying to put Art down, but I just don't think he even brought it off. If he has, it has never come to my attention. (Lunch and Press Briefing, Washington, D.C., Feb. 25, 1981)

Ture admits that a supply-side tax cut will result in "a material expansion in growth and real output compared to what it would otherwise be" and that the inflation rate would also be lower as a result, but "the contribution of increasing output, the *feasible* increase in output to reducing the inflation rate is *relatively small*" (ibid., p. 64; italics supplied). There is one, and only one, way to bring the inflationary rate down permanently and that is through a restrictive monetary policy. In contradistinction to the minimal contribution of classical supply-side fiscal policy to the control of inflation, "the contribution of the Federal Reserve in controlling the rate of growth of monetary aggregates is *relatively enormous*" (ibid., italics supplied). Beryl Sprinkel concurs: "Long-run inflation can only be beaten by restricting the growth of the nation's money supply to match the trend of increase of aggregate production." He goes on to state that although "the budgetary, tax and regulatory portions of [the Reagan administration's] program are designed primarily to stimulate the growth of production . . . [and] real output, this would *contribute only modestly to an easing of inflationary pressures*" (statement before the House Committee on Banking, Finance, and Urban Affairs, July 23, 1981). That is, the output response to the supply-side tax cut would be modest. If so, the Laffer curve goes out the monetarist window—a summary act of defenestration.

It should be clear by now that the classical and monetarist versions of supply-side economics are not complementary. They are at loggerheads. The monetarist school puts the primary emphasis on controlling inflation by restricting the money supply. In the long run, inflation will be permanently cured, interest rates will be low, and output will automatically revert to its "natural" full-employment level. The quantity theory of money triumphs and classical supply-side fiscal policy is to play a subordinate and supportive role. Of itself classical supply-side theory cannot and will not provide a lasting solution. The house of supply-side economics is a troubled one.

V

Neoclassical supply-side theorists have placed all their eggs in the monetarist basket. Having done so, they have turned their backs on the short-run concerns of classical supply-side economists, and the rest of us for that matter. Although classical supply-siders and Keynesians of various persuasions view the workings of the economic system differently, they are both concerned with the problems of the present and the social costs of the current malaise. Members of the monetarist school of supply-side economics, however, have lifted their gaze above the turmoil and have fixed it on the long run where tranquillity will reign if only the rest of us will allow them to put their policies in action. For them, the problem of inflation is paramount and can only be solved by decelerating the money-supply growth rate until it is brought in line with the natural long-term growth rate of the economy. But as we move the monetary growth rate down gradually from an annual rate of 7 percent in 1981 to 3 percent by 1984, what will be the short-run consequences of such an act? "It is naive," Sprinkel tells us, "to expect this deceleration would have no *temporary* adverse effects on income, output and employment." (Senate Budget Committee, Oct. 20, 1981, italics supplied). In the short run, an antiinflationary monetary policy will cause output and employment to fall with little, if any, immediate effect on inflation. But *in the long run,* the economy will be at its natural, full-employment level with no inflation. The short-run effects, in other words, are temporary; they are the price we must pay today for our ultimate salvation. They are "the *unavoidable,* short-run cost of a successful anti-inflationary policy" (italics supplied).

True believers who have a blind faith in the deliverance of tomorrow have been known to bear the pains of today with tranquillity. And in those few instances where they have achieved power, they have not been reluctant to inflict pain on the mass of people—for their own long-run good. It is a most peculiar and comforting view of history. But what if the long run and the short run are not totally independent, and what if their theory, which says that the two can be kept separate, is wrong? What then? If they wreck the economy in the short run, the long-run performance of the economy will be permanently altered. The capital stock, for one, will certainly be lower and with it the long-run ability of the economy to produce. It takes a lot of faith in one's theory to argue that the short-run social costs and the suffering they entail can be ignored. What happens in the short run has in many cases a profound effect on the long-run trajectory of an economy. What we are being told by the Tures and the Sprinkels of this world is: Trust us, we know the truth! But, in the opinion of one observer, "whatever the implications of the policies for the long-run potential of the economy, the effects of these policies in the short run on unemployment and output are real costs that must be balanced against the gains in terms of reduced inflation over future periods. If so, a policy of fixed targets for the growth rate of the money supply at all costs becomes inappropriate."[6] What we are being told by the monetarist school of supply-side economics is that there is an acceptable trade-off between short-term real costs that are transitory and a long-term deliverance that is guaranteed—according to *their* Bible.

And what does their Bible say? As we saw in Chapter 3, it says that the rate of inflation is uniquely dependent on the rate of growth of the money supply in such a way that, if we reduce the monetary growth rate to the natural growth rate of the economy, the rate of inflation will be reduced to zero. When we have done that, all sorts of goodies will follow because the nominal rate of interest is also dependent on the rate of inflation, which places a premium over and above the underlying real rate of interest. With inflation solved, the nominal interest rate will fall to its natural level. But if the nominal interest rate moves in tandem with the expected rate of inflation and the rate of inflation is determined by the money growth rate, then it follows that the nominal interest rate is *positively* related to the money growth rate. We come out of all this with the remarkable proposition that *tight money causes interest rates to fall and, conversely, easy money causes them to rise*—in the long run, of course. Therefore, if investment is highly responsive to interest rates, as monetarists believe, output will reach its natural full-employment rate as well. In summary, by reducing the money growth rate to its appropriate level, we will have simultaneously solved in one fell swoop the two key problems of inflation and unemployment, as well as a host of subsidiary ones. Stagflation will be forever banished from the scene.

But that is not all. Wage rates are also dependent on price-level expectations. Thus, by controlling the money growth rate we reduce wage-rate increases to the noninflationary growth rate of labor's productivity and there is no need for an incomes policy to control inflation. By setting the money growth rate equal to the natural growth rate everything falls into place: wages, interest rates, prices, employment, and growth. It is all so conveniently simple.

There is an awful lot riding on the money supply. It is an awesome burden to put on *one* variable. In doing so, however, the monetary supply-siders have rejected the Laffer canon of classical supply-side theory. It becomes impossible to meld the two into one harmonious theory. They are irreconcilable. Indeed, they are two warring factions, and this has led to a greater problem—the attempt of the Reagan administration to work both sides of the supply-side street while at the same time being counseled by a triumvirate of Old Guard Republican conservatives who believe that the budget should be balanced, at all costs. We turn now to the contradictions of supply-side *praxis*.

Notes

[1] Ture's career at the Treasury began on a stormy note. On January 21, 1981, one week after his appointment, he arranged for the award of a $230,000 noncompetitive Treasury contract to the Washington, D.C., accounting firm of Coopers and Lybrand for a supply-side economic forecasting model. What he did not disclose was that the model was developed by him and sold to Coopers and Lybrand for $60,000. Although the initial arrangement for the sale had been started *five days* before his January 21 appointment to the Treasury, payment was executed on February 2, twelve days after his appointment. The fact remains that he had failed to disclose his financial interest in the model and was found to be in technical violation of the conflict-of-interest laws by the U.S. Inspector General. Although legally culpable, he got off with a mild reprimand and was allowed to keep the $60,000 (*New York Times*, October 12, 1981).

[2] Ture's views, as expressed in this paper, are repeated in virtually all of his testimony before congressional committees and in his press conferences and television interviews on supply-side themes. All quotations, unless otherwise noted, are from his IRET paper.

[3] The latter two, of course, being his mentors at the University of Chicago. On the subject of mentors, the following should be of interest. Shortly after Ture left the presidency of IRET for the Treasury, the name of David C. Raboy appeared on the masthead of IRET as Director of Research. In Raboy's IRET paper (n.d.), "Supply Side Economics—Myths and Realities" (lifted whole from Ture's paper), we find the following (p. 10, italics supplied): " 'Supply-

side' economics incorporates the teachings of the classical economists from Adam Smith to Alfred Marshall to Milton Friedman *and to Norman Ture.*" Becker has been dropped for Marshall—not a bad idea—and Ture has been added, after Friedman, to represent the pinnacle of contemporary economic thought—a very bad idea. It is also clear that the distinction between classical and neoclassical economics has become somewhat fudged by Raboy.

[4]Quotations from Sprinkel are taken from his testimony before various congressional committees, interviews, and press conferences in 1981.

[5]For a wickedly funny dismissal of the Laffer curve, see Martin Gardiner, "Mathematical Games: The Laffer Curve and Other Laughs in Current Economics," *Scientific American*, December 1981, pp. 18-31.

[6]Catherine Hill, "Monetarism and Supply-Side Economics in the United Kingdom" (p. 82, italics supplied), in *Monetary Policy, Selective Credit Policy, and Industrial Policy in France, Britain, West Germany and Sweden: A Staff Study*, Joint Economic Committee, Congress of the United States, June 26, 1981.

CHAPTER 5

Supply-Side Praxis

I

So far we have looked at the two major "schools" of supply-side *theory*. But what about supply-side *praxis*, and the unity of theory and praxis, given that the theoreticians themselves are in fundamental disagreement? How well does Reaganomics adhere to one or the other school, and to what extent does it straddle their inconsistencies adding, in the process, to the general confusion? Unlike supply-side theory, Reaganomics is a political animal catering to different constituencies, and one of its major constituencies is the old praetorian Republican guard consisting of former members of the Eisenhower, Nixon, and Ford administrations with the young Director of the Office of Management and Budget, David Stockman, serving as their reprieved mole in the White House corridors of power.

It was with much fanfare on February 18, 1981, one month after the president's inauguration, that Reagan's *Program for Economic Recovery* was released—the NEP (*New Economic Policy*) for our time from the other side of the political spectrum. It began with a clarion supply-side call to arms. It proclaimed a national recovery program to "rekindle the Nation's entrepreneurial instincts and creativity" by reducing tax burdens in order to revitalize the work ethic and increase private savings and investment. By so liberating the private sector we would find that economic growth would increase by leaps and bounds, promoting at one and the same time increased employment and lower inflation. Stagflation would be forever banished. Releasing the "creativity and ambition of the American people" required, however, a drastic reduction in the role of government. It was big government, in the form of big taxation and even bigger government spending leading to ever-rising deficits, that had sapped the vitality of American capitalism. A revival of the incentives to work and save could not take place without the unraveling of government as we have known it over the past half-century.

The administration's "comprehensive program" consisted of four parts: (1) a drastic reduction in the growth of federal expenditures, (2) a significant reduction in federal tax rates, (3) a severe pruning of federal regulations controlling business, and (4) a monetary policy compatible with the government's new program. The last required "a predictable and steady growth in the money supply." On the face of it, Reaganomics simultaneously embraced the tax cut of classical supply-siders *and* the automatic monetary rule of the monetarist school. A year later, as we shall see, it got caught between the two and turned against the Federal Reserve, making it the scapegoat for its failures.

But even at this early stage, the Reagan administration leaned more heavily toward classical supply-side theory. Inflation is not simply a matter of the money supply climbing erratically over the time series. The *primary* cause of inflation is "uncontrolled government spending . . . , the tendency of government to take an ever-larger share of . . . resources, . . . [and] *excessive deficit spending*" (pp. III:11-12, italics supplied).[1] "In spite of the role played by food and energy prices in recent inflationary outbursts," we are told, "it is misleading to concentrate on these transitory factors as fundamental causes of inflation in the American economy" (p. III:4). Large deficits and easy money have been the major contributors to persistent high inflation.

High marginal tax rates, by discouraging the private incentive to work, save, and invest, have held back the growth of the economy and hence the tax revenues of the government—as have the thousands of pages in the Federal Register which list an ever-proliferating array of complex business regulations. And the even greater proliferation of government expenditures and the deficits they entail co-opt resources better left to the private sector. Since the government's purchase of goods and services, as a proportion of GNP, has been relatively stable over the postwar period, it is the well-meaning but misguided growth in government transfer payments that is the root cause of the problem. These payments require incentive-eroding taxes to finance them and pump purchasing power into the hands of idle recipients. With output less than it would otherwise be and with the purchasing power of the idle poor artificially maintained, it comes as no surprise to the Reagan administration that the deficits of earlier administrations have led to high unemployment and high inflation. Stagflation is the price to be paid for runaway government expenditures and the high taxes they require, with the latter failing to generate balancing revenues by virtue of slowing the rate of economic growth. And with the inflation-induced bracket creep of progressive income taxation, many "households respond . . . by reducing their work effort," giving a further twist to the inflationary spiral—or so the argument goes.

There can be no doubt concerning the Reagan administration's theory of inflation. It is "uncontrolled government spending that has been the primary cause of the sustained high rate of inflation" (p. III:10). And to nail the matter once and for all, *"excessive deficit spending has been the major contributor to the initiation and persistence of inflation"* (p. III:12, italics supplied). Deficits, not the money supply, are the primary cause of inflation. If so, the solution is simple. Cut taxes *and* government expenditures—*and* balance the budget. The latter should not be difficult *if* the cut in taxes so stimulates the incentive to work, along with savings and investment, that the spurt in output will offset, if not actually reverse, the initial fall in government revenues—our old friend, the Laffer curve. If the offset, however, is only partial, a deeper cut in government (transfer) expenditures will be required if the budget is to be balanced, and a deeper one still if the offset is nonexistent. If, however, the Laffer curve has its expected supply-side effect, we have pie in the sky. The fall in expenditures required to balance the budget will be, at worst, minimal. That does not mean, however, that real, inflation-adjusted transfer payments will be maintained. On the contrary, they must be cut if the idle poor are to be converted from yapping kennel dogs into foraging hunting dogs. By cutting transfer payments, moreover, we will be able to reallocate the funds to MX missile systems, B-2 bombers, and all the other accoutrements of the Defense Department, that implacable and insatiable guardian of our national security. That we are in a position of nuclear overkill many times over is beside the point. The technological imperatives of a runaway arms race are boundless. The balance of terror has become as unbalanced as those who have unbalanced it.

II

At any rate, the solution to inflation, low growth, and unemployment is to release the tax brakes—especially on the productive rich—in order to induce harder work and increased savings and investment. All our problems are to be solved by the strict adherence to the supply-side fiscal-policy recommendations of the classicists. But what of the policy prescriptions of the monetarist supply-siders? Monetary policy, in the Reagan game plan, is to play a subordinate, supporting role. Given that government spending, deficits, and the crowding out of the private sector are the primary causes of inflation, excessive money-supply bursts compound inflation, thus further driving up wages and interest rates since both are dependent on the rate of inflation, which, in turn, according to the quantity theory of money, depends on the long-run growth rate of the money supply relative to the natural long-run growth path of real output.

The Reagan administration's monetary scenario, however, is a bit circumspect. An unduly restrictive monetary policy creates "uncertainty [and] undermines long-term investment decisions and economic growth"—presumably by leading to counterproductive high interest rates. If easy money leads to inflation and overly tight money to deflation, then what we need is the "right" monetary policy, one right smack in the middle of the two extremes. What we need, therefore, is a "steady, gradual reduction [of money and credit growth rates] over a period of years," which will make it possible "to reduce inflation substantially and *permanently*" (p. III:22, italics supplied)—which is about as monetarist as one can get.

By having monetary policy focus "on long-term objectives, the resultant restraint on credit and growth would *interact* with the tax and expenditure proposals to lower inflation as well as interest rates" (italics supplied). On the face of it, the classical and monetarist versions of supply-side economics seem to be harmonious. With the two working in tandem, the monetarist supply-siders riding on the rear seat of the bicycle-built-for-two and pumping in support of the front-riding classical supply-siders, the economy will proceed along its steady noninflationary growth path. With the problem of inflation solved, interest rates will settle down to their real rate (based on productivity and thrift in the real sector of the economy), wages will be kept in line with increases in the productivity of labor, and the economy will be in a dynamic state of full employment thanks to the incentive effects of the classical supply-side tax cuts—specifically designed to increase the productive capacity of the economy. According to the administration's Economic Recovery Plan (ERP), Friedman's monetary rule is to be followed so that with a move to "a 4 to 5% annual growth path through 1986 . . . the general rate of inflation . . . [will] decline to less than 5% annually" (p. III:24).

The hope, of course, is that the restricted money supply, in the short run, will not undermine the tax-cut effects of classical supply-side fiscal policy by offsetting them or causing an actual drop in real output, with unemployment rising in the latter case. As the Staff Report of the Congressional Budget Office (CBO) observes, "previous attempts to reduce inflation with tight money have initially resulted in higher unemployment and decreased output, and only subsequently in lower inflation . . . *after a lag of perhaps five to ten years*" (p. 11; italics supplied).[2] The CBO goes on to conclude that "it is by no means certain that monetary policy—however steadfast and credible—will translate wholly and quickly into reduced inflation" (p. 11). We will return to this theme in a later section.

The CBO notwithstanding, the Reagan administration was confident of its game plan:

> Under new procedures the Federal Reserve adopted in October 1979, the Federal Reserve sets targets for growth of reserves considered to be consistent with the desired expansion in the monetary aggregates. Interest rates are allowed to vary over a much wider range in response to changes in the demand for money and credit (p. III:22).

By the end of 1981, this statement would come back to haunt the Reagan administration.

Although the February 1981 ERP of the Reagan administration went far in embracing the classical school of supply-side economics, it was not in full compliance. As announced early in the tenure of the administration, its first order of business was to reduce the "high marginal tax rates on business and individuals [which] discourage work, innovation, and investment necessary to improve productivity and long-run growth" (p. III:4). The second order of business was to cut nondefense expenditures drastically. On tax matters the Reagan administration agreed with the classical supply-siders that high marginal tax rates reduce work effort and that the "tax system has been the key cause of our stagflation" (p. III:6). There was also agreement that cuts in the progressive marginal tax rates on *personal* income should be skewed in favor of the rich—who do most of the saving and investment. But Reaganite praxis also called for sharp cuts in the business corporate income tax, greater investment tax credits for business, and accelerated depreciation (the 10-5-3 plan). Here, Reaganomics parted company with classical supply-side economics.

Progressivity in tax rates, argues Wanniski, applies to business "to a limited degree."[3] It is mostly *individuals* who are sensitive to inflation-induced bracket creep. And it is individuals and individualistic venture capitalists who constitute the driving force behind a dynamic capitalism. Gilder and Kemp (who received a strong assist from Wanniski in the writing of his book) are clear on this point. First the "radical" Kemp.[4]

> [C]onfining most tax relief to retained corporate profits, through such devices as accelerated depreciation or an investment tax credit, *keeps capital locked into established firms.* By focusing on the *individual* investor, on the other hand, we can stimulate risk investment in innovative *new* firms that are the main source of *new* products and *new* technologies.

Gilder, the other "radical," is equally outspoken on the issue:

> Investment tax credits and rapid depreciation allowances— although better than no tax cuts at all— tend to favor the recreation of current capital stock rather than the creation of new forms of capital and modes of production.[5]

Classical supply-side theorists prefer cuts in personal income taxes and in capital gains taxes (which, according to Kemp, "give investors the incentive to buy shares with low current dividends but good, though risky, potential for growth" (p. 67) rather than the cutting of corporate income taxes (which are proportional for the larger firms) and the granting of investment tax credits and accelerated depreciation allowances (which also favor the bigger firms). It is clear that Reagan is not a purist. He has many friends in big business and is not as "radical" as Kemp or Gilder. Thus tax relief for business, with investment tax credits and accelerated depreciation, was included in his program. He does agree, however, on the need to dismantle the welfare state.

The cuts in nondefense spending will do wonders for the work incentives of the poor (according to classical supply-side theory). There were to be cuts (which were later implemented) in Medicaid, child nutrition programs, certain Social Security benefits, food stamps, unemployment benefits, youth training and employment programs, public service employment, income-assistance payments (AFDC), and a whole medley of other social-service programs as well. The geographic distribution of these cuts is almost certain to hit the already depressed Northeast and Midwest harder than the Sunbelt states. On the other hand, defense expenditures, according to the CBO Staff Report, were scheduled in the first round to increase *in real terms* between 1980 and 1984 by an annual average of 7 percent, compared to a nondefense spending rate of growth of 1 percent *in nominal terms*. Real nondefense spending would be 15 percent lower in 1984 than in 1980 (see Staff Report, p. xiv). And here is a problem for supply-side theorists.

The Kemp-Roth 25 percent cut in taxes on personal income, to be phased in over a three-year period, plus the revenue cost of faster tax depreciation of capital expenditures, will approximately *offset* the inflation-induced income tax increase (bracket creep)[6] together with the scheduled rise in Social Security taxes. Furthermore, the nondefense cuts will be diverted to finance the planned jump in defense expenditures. In effect, there will be no real tax cut, merely the suppression of bracket creep, and no substantive decrease in overall government expenditures—although there will be an enormous redistribution of the social product in favor of the rich. Supply-side *praxis* has apparently left supply-side *theory* in the lurch. *In practice, the administration's program is a massive redistribution gambit with a reverse twist, not a growth scenario based on classical supply-side theory.*

What then about the Laffer curve and our position on it? If there is, in effect, no net real tax cut, then we are stuck on its upper reaches—where classical supply-side theorists are convinced we are. The President's *Program* (which makes no mention of the Laffer curve) will have been aborted.

It seems fairly clear that supply-side praxis and classical supply-side theory are in collision, between the claim of lowering the real tax rate and the reality of merely neutralizing the effect of inflation bracket creep and the rise in Social Security taxes. Of course, supply-side practitioners will always have Congress or the Federal Reserve to blame if things don't work out exactly right, and supply-side theorists will be able to squirm *their* way out—taxes weren't really cut or not cut enough, or the money supply was not properly managed by the Federal Reserve. Both practitioners and theorists have their escape hatches ready.

III

The Reagan administration is engaged in what it calls "A New Beginning." The people should be set free, the "workers, managers, savers, investors, buyers, and sellers . . . who make up the economy." And one thing the "people" *don't* need is "the government to make reasoned and intelligent decisions about how to best organize and run their own lives. The most appropriate role for government economic policy is to provide a stable and unfettered environment in which private individuals can confidently plan and make appropriate decisions" (p. III:24). And the best way to do that, as we have seen, is by personal and business tax reductions, reductions in government spending, the elimination of unneeded government regulations over business, *and the pursuit of a stable monetary policy.* Again, the straddle between the two major schools of supply-side economics (p. III:24):

> A stable monetary policy, gradually slowing growth rates of money and credit along a preannounced and predictable path, will lead to reductions in inflation. At the same time, the effects of supply-oriented tax and regulatory changes on working incentives, expansion and improvement of the capital stock, and improved productivity will boost output.

In the heady early days of the Reagan administration, caution was thrown to the wind and these theses, supported by "hard" data, were nailed against the doors of Congress. Belief in the model was absolute, or so it appeared publicly. Do as we say and all will be well. We know, and here are the figures to prove it. Tables abounded which showed that everything would work as expected. Under this public-relations onslaught, Congress retreated and gave the President virtually everything he wanted—and then some, as congressmen of both parties tacked on tax reductions above and beyond the call of duty for their favorite constituencies, while emasculating the system of social transfer payments laboriously built up over the past fifty years. Those were the days of euphoria.

Annual Growth Rates, the Rate of Interest, the Rate of Unemployment, and the Federal Deficit: 1981-86

	1981	1982	1983	1984	1985	1986
Annual rate of inflation ($\dot{P}$)	9.9	8.3	7.0	6.0	5.4	4.9
Annual real GNP growth rate ($\dot{Q}$)	1.1	4.2	5.0	4.5	4.2	4.2
Annual nominal GNP growth rate ($\dot{Y}=\dot{P}+\dot{Q}$)	11.0	12.5	12.0	10.5	9.6	9.1
Money growth rate ($\dot{M}$)	7.0	6.0	5.0	4.0	3.0	2.0
Velocity growth rate ($\dot{V}$)	4.0	6.5	7.0	6.5	6.6	7.1
91-day TB rate	11.1%	8.9%	7.8%	7.0%	6.0%	5.6%
Unemployment rate	7.8%	7.2%	6.6%	6.4%	6.0%	5.6%
Fiscal year federal deficit ($billion)	−$55	−$45	−$23	+$1	+$6	+$28

The accompanying table lists the projected rates of inflation and real GNP growth from 1981 to 1986, as well as the administration's projections for the rate of interest on 91-day Treasury bills (TBs) and the expected rates of unemployment over the same time period. The nominal GNP growth rate, using the dynamic form of the quantity equation ($\dot{P}+\dot{Q}=\dot{Y}$), corresponds, roughly, to the administration's own estimates. Although the administration called for the adoption of the monetarist rule for controlling the money supply, no detailed scenario was provided. The money growth rates shown in the table are based on Beryl Sprinkel's July 23, 1981, *Statement before the House Committee on Banking, Finance, and Urban Affairs*, in which he called for "the phased deceleration of money supply growth which we presented in February—M1B [currency plus all checking deposits] growth rate of 7% in 1981 and 1% less each year through 1986," in the belief that such a phased deceleration would result in the "elimination of inflationary pressures."[7] The table's velocity growth rates, however, are *derived* from the equation $\dot{V} = \dot{Y} - \dot{M}$. They appear nowhere in the President's February 1981 ERP report—and that is where the problem lies. Somebody at the Office of Management and Budget wasn't doing his homework. The figures did not add up—as David Stockman was later to admit—and the Congressional Budget Office was quick to pick up the blooper.

If the real rate of economic growth is to be increased almost four-fold from 1981 to 1986 (from 1.1 to 4.2 percent) while we are sharply reducing the money supply growth rate (from 7 to 2 percent), then the growth rate of velocity, as the table shows, would have to increase from 4.0 in 1981 to 7.1 in 1986. Given a nominal 1981 GNP of $2,900 billion and a $430 billion money supply, the velocity of money (Y/M) would have to increase from 6.7 in 1981 to 9.1 in 1986 in order to finance the administration's projected real GNP growth rate of 4.2 percent at a 4.9 percent inflation rate.[8]

The problem is that the administration predicted a *fall* in the interest rate (91-day TBs) from 11.1 percent in 1981 to 5.6 in 1986. It did so on the basis of a convenient belief—that interest rates "are largely a mirror of price expectations." If Sprinkel's monetary rule is followed and the money growth rate is reduced, then, according to the quantity theory of money, the rate of inflation will be reduced—from 9.9 percent in 1981 to 4.9 percent in 1986. And since the nominal interest rate, given the real rate of interest, reflects in full the rate of inflation, the interest rate will also fall, according to the administration's model, from 11.1 percent in 1981 to a low of 5.6 percent in 1986. The problem is that the model implicitly assumes a falling rate of interest *and* a rising income velocity of money. This cannot be. Velocity, as the CBO was quick to point out, is supposed to be "a rough measure of the demand for money relative to supply" (p. 10), with the interest rate representing the price of money. But then how can an excess demand for money lead to a *fall* in its price? It's all very confusing, especially when such a muddled argument is propounded by an administration which trumpets the workings of demand and supply in a free market system. The administration's model was internally inconsistent.

But there were other problems as well. The model predicted a sharply declining rate of unemployment and an equally sharp fall in the federal deficit, with the budget not only balanced but in surplus from 1984 on—1984 being the end of Reagan's first term in office. On the first anniversary of the Reagan administration, in January of 1982, the real growth rate had fallen steadily from 8.6 percent in the first quarter of 1981, on an annual basis, to 1.6 percent in the second quarter, followed by 1.4 percent in the third quarter. The year closed with a numbing −4.7 percent for the fourth quarter—with unemployment rising from 7 percent to almost 9 percent over the course of the year. For calendar 1981, the overall growth rate was 2 percent with negative rates being projected for the first and second quarters of 1982, and an expected unemployment rate of 10 percent by mid-year. If, to use Jack Kemp's favorite borrowed metaphor, "a rising tide lifts all boats," so does an ebbing tide lower them.

At the same time, annual deficits exceeding $100 billion were being projected through at least fiscal 1984. The only part of the scenario that seemed to be moving in the right direction was the inflation rate. By the end of 1981 it had fallen to 8.9 percent and was expected to continue to fall (as indeed it did, to about 4 percent), but the decline had little, if anything, to do with the money supply and it could hardly be attributed to a supply-side spurt in real output. Indeed, with the economy performing at 72 percent of industrial capacity and with large-scale unemployment, wage pressures abated. Moreover, a glut of oil on the world markets kept energy prices down. Bountiful harvests had a similar effect on food prices, and high mortgage rates served to prevent housing prices from going up—all significant components of the consumer price index. The administration could hardly take the credit for such exogenous factors as the oil glut and the good harvest, and it was not about to lay claim to such endogenous factors as the fall in real output, the high unemployment rate, and the high level of interest rates. But there was more wrong with the model than a mere inconsistency concerning the income velocity of money and the rate of interest, or the wrongheadedness of the real world. A hoax had been perpetrated on the American people, and when it was revealed shock waves blew some of the faithful off their feet.

Notes

[1] On the issue of deficit spending and its impact on inflation, Reaganomics changed its mind sharply within the course of a single year. This matter will be explored more fully later.

[2] *An Analysis of President Reagan's Budget Revisions for Fiscal Year 1982: Staff Working Paper, March 1981.* The staff paper is a devastating document which, not surprisingly, caused an uproar in Washington when it came out, with David Stockman of OMB leading the counterattack. Others in the Senate called for Alice Rivlin's resignation as Director of CBO, so far to no avail.

[3] *The Way the World Works*, p. 224.

[4] *An American Renaissance: A Strategy for the 1980's*, pp. 66-67, italics supplied.

[5] *Wealth and Poverty*, p. 243.

[6] It should be noted that under the *Economic Recovery and Tax Act of 1981* the indexation of tax rates will become effective on January 1, 1985, although currently there is a movement to rescind this part of the Act.

[7] Later, on November 3, 1981, in a New York speech before the Open House Meeting of Duff and Phelps, Inc., Sprinkel called "for a gradual reduction in the rate of money growth from the 7.3% increase in 1980 to less than half that by 1985." It is clear in this context that in his July statement Sprinkel meant to say "and 1% *point* less each year," which is how it has been interpreted for purposes of the table—even though it projects a lower than the historical 3 percent long-term growth rate for the American economy.

[8] Without such an increase in velocity, the administration's game plan would be wrecked. The 2 percent money growth rate would serve as a brake and drag the economy down from its projected growth rate. The increase in velocity from 6.7 to 9.1 represents an *indirect* increase in the money supply since any change in velocity can be restated in terms of its *monetary equivalent* by multiplying the base period money supply (M_0) by the percentage change in velocity $\Delta V/V_0$). In this case the monetary equivalent of the velocity change is $M_0(\Delta V/V_0) = \$430\,(2.4/6.7) = \$154$ billion. Without it, the scenario collapses.

CHAPTER 6

The Great Confession and Its Aftermath

I

By the year's end, the administration's scenario was coming apart at the seams. It wasn't going according to plan. It was then that David Stockman's revelations exploded with a force high up on the Richter scale. The figures did not add up and the administration had known it beforehand. It was a hype and Stockman all along had had serious doubts about the glories of supply-side economics. Over a period of nine months, he had poured his heart out to a Washington Post reporter who dutifully revealed all in the December 1981 issue of *The Atlantic*.

Cutting taxes, raising defense expenditures, and balancing the budget were simply incompatible, the President's 1981 ERP Report notwithstanding. The OMB computer, working in the dark of night, had predicted budget deficits unlike those of any previous administration. So . . . the computer was reprogrammed to yield the desired results: rising real output, falling unemployment and interest rates, a sharp decline in the rate of inflation, and a balanced budget. The economy would perform exactly as supply-siders said it would—or else! As Stockman admitted, at the time, "None of us really understands what's going on with all these numbers . . . . People are getting from A to B and it's not clear how they are getting there." In the words of the reporter, William Greider, "Reagan's policy-makers knew that their plan was wrong, or at least inadequate to its promised effects, but the President went ahead and conveyed the opposite impression to the American public." Or, in Stockman's delightfully understated words, "There was a certain dimension of our theory that was unrealistic."

Stockman, from early on, was obsessed with balancing the budget. Losing revenue by cutting taxes required cutting government expenditures to whatever extent necessary to balance the budget. At all costs, expenditures were to be be restricted to the revenues at hand. It was then that Stockman unleashed his proposal for cutting Social Security payments. The political reaction was awesome and the administration beat a hasty retreat by appointing a bipartisan commission, under Alan Greenspan, to study the long-run solution to the system's problems—with the report not due until after the 1982 congressional elections.

Stockman had not been an early advocate of classical supply-side economics. His conversion was later than most and his departure sooner. He had, all along, shared some of the doubts of the monetarist supply-siders concerning the wonders of the Laffer curve. "I've never believed," he confessed to his confessor, "that just cutting taxes alone will cause output and employment to expand." He then went on to admit that the whole classical supply-side tax cut was a fraud, an admission that rattled Washington to its foundations when it was published in *The Atlantic* (italics supplied):

> The hard part of the supply-side tax cut is dropping the top rate from 70 to 50 percent—the rest of it is a secondary matter. The original argument was that the top bracket was too high, and that's having the most devastating effect on the economy. Then, the general argument was that in order to make this a palatable matter, you had to bring down all the brackets. But, I mean, *Kemp-Roth was always a Trojan horse to bring down the top rate.*

. . . .

> It's kind of hard to sell "trickle down," so the supply-side formula was the only way to get a tax policy that was really "trickle down."

Supply-side is "trickle down" theory.

There it was in all its ugly rawness! The Laffer curve was a hype. It provided a smoke screen for a crude raid on the public Treasury by the rich and the powerful. Classical supply-side theorists were simply the stalking horses of a deliberate and cynical hoax. And when the tax bill went before the Congress, the special interests had a field day. The administration's tax bill became a Christmas tree. Special tax concessions and give-aways were added, as Greider related, "for oil-lease holders and real-estate tax shelters, and generous loopholes that virtually eliminated the corporate income tax." Or, as Stockman put it: "Do you realize the greed that came to the forefront? The hogs were really feeding. The greed level, the level of opportunism, just got out of control." According to Greider, "Every tax lobby in town . . . moved in on the legislation, and pet amendments for obscure tax advantage and profit become the pivotal issues of legislative action, not the grand theories of supply-side tax reduction."

With what was added on top of a fraudulent Laffer curve, the budget was left spinning out of control. It could not be balanced. Large deficits were clearly in the works. The administration's model had not only been based on a "theory" that even Stockman knew could not work; it had been sabotaged by the greed of special interests and by a compliant Congress which knew a God-sent opportunity when it saw one. Apart from the doubtful teachings of the Laffer curve, Stockman had been cured of his earlier and brief flirtation with supply-side theory because of its political unreality. In his words:

> [T]he naive supply-siders just missed this whole dimension. You don't stop inflation without some kind of dislocation . . . . Supply-side was the wrong atmospherics—not wrong theory or wrong economics but wrong atmospherics . . . . The supply-siders have gone too far. They created this nonpolitical view of the economy . . . and their happy vision of this world of growth and no inflation with no pain.

Deeply disillusioned, he left his interlocutor with one final bit of widsom: "*Whenever there are great strains or changes in the economic system, it tends to generate crackpot theories, which then find their way into the legislative channels*"—and which are then raped in the process, he might have added, by cynical interest groups and politicians.

II

One must admire Stockman's candor and his ability to learn—and to change. As a student at Michigan State University in the 1960s, by Greider's account, he read Herbert Marcuse, C. Wright Mills, and Paul Goodman and became a leader of the campus radicals against the Vietnam War. Graduating in 1964, he then entered the Harvard Divinity School, but soon dropped his studies in the moral philosophy of Christian activism and turned to the social sciences, though unfortunately not to the field of economics. His new mentors were now such neo-conservative thinkers as James Q. Wilson, Nathan Glazer, and Daniel Patrick Moynihan. Next in his Odyssey to the Right, he became a Republican congressman from his home district in western Michigan. The rest is history as he made his way to the Office of Management and Budget, under Reagan, at the ripe age of 34.

The reaction to his *Atlantic* revelations was swift to come. Said Arthur Laffer: "Stockman has lost his credibility." Said Jude Wanniski: "He slowly turned himself into an opponent . . . . We didn't think he would so rapidly abandon our supply-side fiscal and monetary ideas . . . . The thing that hurt us most was the cynicism." Said Jack Kemp, grandly: "The Reagan program is bigger than any one person." The cruelest cut of all came from Lane Kirkland, president of the AFL-CIO:

> Lest you feel a twinge of human sympathy for his public embarrassment, let me remind you that . . . he was the original interior decorator of this economic house of ill repute. Now that the sirens are sounding and the bust is due, he has his story ready. He was

only the piano player in the parlor. He never knew what was going on upstairs.

The general consensus, among supply-siders, was that Stockman had been working too hard, round the clock, and that he had cracked. But perhaps the only one to have seen what really lay behind Stockman's outpouring was Alan Reynolds, a lesser-known supply-side enthusiast: "He's always been a doubting Thomas. The minute he took office, he became a monomaniacal budget-balancer." That was it! He had never really left the Old Guard Republican traditionalists. His natural allies, all along, were to be found in the President's informal Economic Advisory Board—Arthur "Fluctuations" Burns, former Chairman of the Council of Economic Advisors under Eisenhower, and Chairman of the Federal Reserve Board of Governors under Nixon, who had begun his career measuring business cycles and ended it creating them; George Schultz, Secretary of the Treasury under Nixon; and Herbert Stein and Alan Greenspan, Chairmen of the Council of Economic Advisors under Nixon and Ford, respectively. For this Old Guard, the Laffer curve was indeed a hoax. If the Kemp-Roth tax cut was to be put in place, as it was over their objections and those of the Chairman of the Federal Reserve Board, Paul Volcker, then government expenditures would have to be drastically cut, and even more so if defense expenditures were to increase in real terms. At all costs, the budget had to be balanced. Deficits were anathema. This was where things came apart and led to Stockman's new drive, after having been spared by Reagan for his indiscretions with no more than a trip to the woodshed, to increase tax revenues and cut government social expenditures still further.

The original February 1981 scenario, admittedly doctored, projected a series of declining deficits leading to a surplus in 1984, the end of the President's first term. One month later, the Congressional Budget Office released its projections based on a more realistic model of the economy. Although it, too, showed the deficits declining over the same four fiscal years (1981-84),

Reagan's terminal surplus of $1 billion came out as a $49 billion deficit. The figures in dispute, early in 1981, are shown in the table.

	Estimated Fiscal Year Budgetary Deficits			
	1981	1982	1983	1984
Administration	−$55	−$45	−$23	+$ 1
Congressional Budget Office	−$63	−$67	−$59	−$49

By mid-1981, the economy started to sag on its way to a full-blown recession. By year's end, the sag had become a steep decline in real output accompanied by high unemployment rates. The near-term impact on the deficit was not difficult to figure out. Roughly, the federal deficit increases by $30 billion for each percentage point rise in the unemployment rate—$25 billion for increased federal expenditures on unemployment insurance, food stamps, etc., and $5 billion in lost tax revenues. The administration's early deficit projections and the 1984 surplus were now seen to have been wildly optimistic. The big incentive surge had not yet materialized. The Laffer curve, if it existed at all, was severely lagged. As the January 1982 State of the Union Message and the February submission deadline for the President's budget to Congress (the first one of his administration) drew near, there was a frenzy of activity that barely covered the deep rifts within the administration over the President's economic program.

The Old Guard Advisory Committee and the OMB under Stockman were appalled by the ballooning Federal deficit; it seemed to be on a trajectory of its own. They demanded further cuts in all government expenditures (including the military) and a postponement or stretch-out of the Kemp-Roth tax cuts on *earned* income[1] coupled with an increase in the excise taxes on cigarettes, liquor, and gasoline. Come what may, the budget had to be balanced. Abundant leaks to the press, indicating that taxes would increase, were designed to force the President's hand. Either that or a public-relations job was being mounted to show an embattled President giving in reluctantly to the pressure of his own advisors. A shifting of the blame appeared to be in the works. The President was shown to be fighting for the integrity of his program against the onslaught of Stockman and the Republican Old Guard. The classical supply-siders were in danger of being pushed aside by the budget-balancers.

Powerful Senate and House leaders joined the fray and started talking publicly about the need to delay the 1982-83 tax cuts by three months in order to increase revenues annually by $8 billion. Another $7 billion was to be realized by repealing the deduction for interest on consumer credit, and at least $10 billion annually from increased excise taxes. In addition, a tax on natural gas and imported crude oil could raise an additional $24 billion a year. All told, taxes could increase by $49 billion a year, to be supplemented by at least a $13 billion further reduction in government expenditures over and above the $37 billion reduction of spring 1981—in the nondefense area, of course. As early as mid-October of 1981 talk was of the need for a "mid-course correction." The chief economist from Stockman's OMB, Lawrence A. Kudlow, raised the art of euphemism to new heights. Tax increases were to be known as "revenue enhancement" or "receipts strengthening." Asked the reason for this doublespeak, Mr. Kudlow responded with a disarming frankness: "There is no better way to sell economic theory than by the euphemistic route."

Euphemism, however, had nothing to do with the next development in this unfolding saga. The President retreated to the isolation of Camp David to think his way through. What he had to think about was the new deficit projections of his Council of Economic Advisors and the Office of Management and Budget—$109 billion in fiscal 1982, $152 billion in 1983, and $162 billion in 1984, assuming no tax increases or postponements and no further spending cuts. The Senate's projections were even worse—$165 billion in fiscal 1983, $215 billion in 1984, $252 billion in 1985, and a whopping $299 billion in 1986. In view of the impending disaster, David Stockman demanded tax increases on the order of $60 to

$80 billion over the next three years.

It looked like the Old Guard budget-balancers were going to have their way, but they underestimated the tenacity of the classical supply-siders. Jack Kemp, as befits a one-time come-from-behind quarterback, led the counterattack in early January 1982. He accused the President's men of rigging their deficit estimates—by now a familiar charge applied in reverse—in order to stampede the President into undoing his tax cuts. Kemp then announced that he would be meeting with the President in a week's time in order to strengthen the President's resolve and to guarantee his theoretical purity. Whether or not the President would opt for "revenue enhancement," one thing was clear. He would not undo his three-year 25 percent tax cut on earned income (the Trojan horse was to be saved) or, for that matter, the more immediate cuts on investment income. Still, the supply-siders opposed *any* increase in other taxes despite the fact that key supply-siders believed that excise taxes, unlike personal income taxes, had little, if any, effect on incentives. Jack Kemp, preparing for his meeting with the President, was adamant:

> I have been assured that decisions are not locked in. Douglas MacArthur once said that the councils of war breed timidity and defeatism. The forces of timidity are having their hour, but I have hope the President will decide the right thing in the end.

With General MacArthur on the scene, in spirit, the battle was joined and Jack Kemp's hopes, as things turned out, were well placed—despite the defection of the Secretary of the Treasury, Donald T. Regan, from the ranks of the classical supply-siders and the rumblings of the Chairman of the Federal Reserve Board of Governors, Paul Volcker, who was aghast at the size of the projected deficits and their potential impact on the financial sector. The U.S. Chamber of Commerce galloped to Kemp's rescue in the nick of time as did prominent leaders of major corporations. And the Gallup poll made clear that the public would not tolerate any postponement of their tax cuts or any increase in excise taxes on their treasured vices.

The President was caught in an insoluble dilemma. He could not have his tax cuts and balance the budget, too. He had to make a choice. Indeed, the tax cuts were themselves the direct cause of his deficits, with a strong assist from the downturn of the economy. The President finally decided to remain true to his supply-side convictions. Jack Kemp had carried the day. There would be no "revenue enhancement" or "receipts strengthening," nor would the original tax cuts be altered in any way. Let the deficits mount! Deficits, the President now said, were "a necessary evil." After all, both supply-side schools had never been as exercised about deficits as the Old Guard had been—and was. For classical supply-siders, there was always the Laffer curve, and for monetarist supply-siders it was the money supply, not the size of the deficit, that really mattered.

In February 1982 the President took the plunge officially. He sent his budget to Congress with a projected $92 billion deficit for fiscal 1983 alone (which was later raised to $96 billion because of unexpected increases in the cost of farm price supports). Even this estimate was suspect since it assumed a 3 percent growth rate for 1982 and 5.2 percent for 1983, with unemployment *falling* from 7.2 to 5.5 percent over the same time period. It also assumed a sharp drop in interest rates to 10.5 percent in 1983. Moreover, the budget assumed a second round of cuts in social expenditures to the tune of $13 billion—$2.5 billion in Medicare, $2 billion in Medicaid, $2.4 billion in food stamps, and so on up to and including student loans, federal retirement funds, child nutrition programs, and supplemental security income payments for the retired and the poor. In addition, another $14.2 billion was to be cut from education, employment training programs, transportation, subsidized housing, etc. Meanwhile, of course, nominal defense expenditures for fiscal 1983 were to *rise* by $33.1 billion, or by 18.1 percent. In effect, the poor were to finance the increased military budget while the rich ran to their banks with their tax savings. Still, the 1983 deficit was to be $92 billion, followed by $83 billion in 1984 and $72 billion in 1985. Said the President, on

February 9, 1982, in a speech before the Iowa legislature, "*We have in place an economic program that is based on sound economic theory . . . . We have faith in our program and we are sticking with it.*" And to his detractors, he added, "Let me say as politely as I can, 'Put up or shut up.' We have a solid plan already in place." The supply-siders had won the day. The Old Guard had been put to rout. Budget-balancing was not a first priority. Deficits could well be tolerated. The Laffer curve would attend to them—in due time.

Private sector deficit estimates by banks, brokerage houses, and economic consultant firms were not long in coming. They far exceeded the administration's estimates. For fiscal 1983, they averaged $117 billion, compared to the administration's $92 billion estimate.[2] Even Alan Greenspan, a key member of the President's unofficial Advisory Board, put the figure at $120 billion. No one believed the President's projections, including the stock market, which promptly tumbled to new lows in February. The reasons for disbelieving the administration by people normally sympathetic to conservative economic policies lay in the underlying assumptions of the administration's new model. They were simply not credible. The administration was seen to be engaged, one year later and after Stockman's confession, in a new round of dissembling. The President was forced to retreat to a remarkable second line of defense—remarkable, considering the confidence with which the original February 1981 plan was foisted upon the country. "I don't think," he argued, "that any economist would disagree, but there are so many imponderables that no one can project the future more than the immediate year." In the long run, in other words, maybe the problem would disappear, but it was the President's projection for the "immediate" year that was causing so much consternation.

But why this outcry over the short-run size of the deficit? Supply-side economists of both the classical and monetarist stripe did not regard it as the central problem. Indeed, some supply-siders sounded like unrepentant Keynesians when they argued that the deficit should be viewed not in absolute terms but relatively as a proportion of GNP, and that in this light there was no real problem.[3] The fact was that the President's massive $836 billion cumulative five-year tax cut was a major contributor to the deficits. Wall Street, Republican conservatives, and the business community at large were convinced that the magnitude of the projected deficits would lead to inflation,[4] high interest rates, and a further drop in real output and employment.

It should be kept in mind, however, that it was to the classical supply-siders that the President had turned for succor, and it was they who took up the cudgels in his defense. The *monetarist* supply-siders were not-so-strangely mute, for it was their version of supply-side economics that the conservative opponents of the President were implicitly using against him. And it is to this split in the supply-side ranks that we now turn.

III

By the end of the first week in February 1982, the U.S. Treasury came into the financial markets with $20 billion of short- and long-term issues in order to raise $6.7 billion in new cash. And to cover the first quarter 1982 deficit, they would shortly need to raise an additional $41.25 billion in new cash. The government interest rate promptly shot up to 14 percent, despite the overall poor performance of the economy. And things would be getting considerably worse with the deficits projected for fiscal 1983 and 1984 in the pipeline—even if they were as small as the wildly conservative estimates of the administration, which are believed by no one. In the view of the street-wise financial community, the deficits would lead to a resumption of inflation with unemployment rising at the same time—a further turn of the stagflation screw. To put it briefly, the administration was hoist with its own monetarist "crowding-out" petard.

The need to finance the monumental Reagan deficits—more than the combined deficits of the Eisenhower, Kennedy, Johnson, Nixon, Ford, and Carter administrations—would crowd out the private sector and cause a decline in real output, leading to *second-*

ary increases in the deficits above and beyond the administration's own highly conservative projections. With the economy saving 5 to 6 percent of GNP and the government borrowing 15 percent, the deficits would gobble up goods and services without adding to their supply. Interest rates would soar, possibly to 16 or 20 percent, as would business bankruptcies. At least this was the view of major elements of the banking and business communities in the first quarter of 1982.

The crowding-out effect followed from the low money-supply growth rate to which the administration was pledged. The deficits were not to be monetized. The President had been backed into a supply-side corner. The 1981 tax cuts were supposed to generate a marked increase in the saving ratio which would "automatically" spill over into new investment leading to increases in output and employment which, of themselves, would generate new tax revenues (the Laffer-curve effect) to reduce the deficits. But now the administration was caught in the position of sopping up the expected increases in savings, should they come about, in order to finance the deficits. Output would therefore not grow. And if the expected increase in savings did not materialize, which was more probable, real output would fall giving the lie, in either case, to the administration's projected 5.5 percent growth rate for fiscal 1983.

The President had two choices: (1) either maintain the classical supply-side tax cuts and incur large deficits, or (2) bring the budget into balance by undoing the tax cuts while at the same time increasing "revenue enhancing" excise taxes. He chose the first and was impaled on the crowding-out hypothesis of the monetarist school. There was a third alternative: reduce the projected increase in defense expenditures. That, however, was totally unacceptable to the President. With defense expenditures soaring, with the Laffer-curve effect in a shambles, with a significant second round of cuts in nondefense expenditures highly doubtful for political as well as humanitarian reasons, and with the policy of monetary restraint in place, it is not at all surprising that the federal deficit was out of control. The President's options were severely restricted. He would not give up his misguided classical supply-side convictions, his dark view of the Soviet Union would not permit the restraint of defense expenditures, and he had pretty much reached the bottom of the barrel in nondefense expenditure cuts. *The only thing left was the money supply,* plus a diversionary tactic called the "New Federalism."

It did not take long to launch an attack on the Federal Reserve system, which, being independent of the executive branch of government, became a convenient patsy. Tight money in the face of large deficits causes interest rates to mount and output and employment to fall—thus offsetting the effects of Lafferite supply-side economics, assuming it is an accurate description of reality to begin with, which it is not. In monetarist terms, however, if nominal interest rates are a markup over the inflation rate, and if the inflation rate is uniquely dependent on the growth rate of the money supply, then a steady decrease in the money supply should bring down prices and thus the rates of interest. But the crowding-out hypothesis, which is itself predicated on a restricted money supply in order to avoid a monetization of the public debt, assures that the deficits will lead to increasing, not falling, interest rates. The argument is really over the long run versus the short run. The monetarist Nirvana is definitely long run. The rest of us, however, are doomed to live in the short run and with its problems—politicians even more so than others, for their very life as politicians depends on their reactions to the short-run problems of society, especially just before elections.

The Federal Reserve system under its chairman, Paul Volcker, is under the monetarist sway. In October 1979, the Federal Reserve announced a shift of policy. The policy target would no longer be the pattern of interest rates. Instead, the Federal Reserve would henceforth focus almost exclusively on controlling monetary aggregates, with interest rates free to gyrate in response to competitive market forces. The policy shift was seen as the sole answer to the problem of inflation. But the shift now flew in the face of *classical* supply-side fiscal policy. It threatened to undo the beneficial effects of the supply-side tax cut. Not surprisingly, the President and the Secretary of the Treasury, Donald T. Regan, began voicing criticisms of the Federal Reserve and blaming it for the high interest rates that were thwarting the administration's economic policies. The criticism, however, underwent a series of transmutations. Early in the Reagan administration, the criticism was that the Federal Reserve was not tight enough. Later the Federal Reserve was accused of being too tight, and now the argument became that it was too erratic in its control over the money supply, causing confusion in the financial markets.[5] The entire gamut of possibilities had been run.

One of the leading monetarist supply-siders, Beryl Sprinkel, insisted that it was not the deficits that were causing the interest rates to climb, but the *volatility* of the money supply. He obviously had forgotten his oft-touted argument of the crowding-out effect. The classical supply-siders, on the other hand, called for an easing of the Federal Reserve's tight money policy. Volcker was adamant. As long as the budget remained unbalanced, the Federal Reserve would continue with its policy of monetary restraint.

Jack Kemp was quick to attack. The current recession was to be laid squarely on Paul Volcker. It was the high interest rates that were choking the economy and counteracting the fiscal policy of classical supply-side economics. "There has to be a change," he warned, "in Federal Reserve policy to get the interest rates down." And the only way to do that would be to make interest rates the policy target and ease up on the money supply. But then, according to the monetarist branch, this would cause prices to increase with interest rates in tow since interest rates are a markup over the rate of inflation. "I am very concerned," Volcker counterpunched, "about the deficit . . . . If the government is going to stand out there and pre-empt a very large share of the savings flow, you call into question what financial market conditions will look like out there in 1983 and 1984." For Volcker, obviously, high interest rates are the result of large deficits. Jude Wanniski, a charter member of the classical supply-side school, joined the fray:

> Last year was the year of fiscal policy and we succeeded in putting our fiscal policy in place. *Now we have to move to the second*

stage, and that means getting rid of monetarism, which is the thing that's standing in the way of recovery. The basic inconsistency in Reaganomics is having a contractionary monetary policy and an expansionary fiscal policy; it dooms us to stalemate.

....

If we could *target* lower interest rates, the stock and bond markets would certainly revive and unemployment would be down. By the end of the year a shift in monetary policy could mean the difference between unemployment rates of 10 percent and 7 percent.[6]

Alan Greenspan, one of the leaders of the budget-balance school, put it another way (italics supplied):

A necessary condition for the President's program to succeed is that long-term interest rates must come down somewhat. *The critical issue is not monetary policy, but fiscal policy.* If the President can alter spending and tax receipts to reduce the deficit to $100 billion, the implication will be that the deficit is no longer out of control, and I think long rates will fall.[7]

Greenspan is for undoing Wanniski's supply-side tax cut!

IV

Where does supply-side *praxis* come out in all this? It is clear that there is a lack of coherence in supply-side "theory." The classical supply-siders are in fundamental disagreement with their monetarist brethren, and the Old Guard budget-balancers are undercutting both. Supply-side praxis is based on a garbled "theory" which points in several directions at the same time. Whichever of the two supply-side schools one subscribes to, there is no convincing evidence to support the "theory" unless one doctors the data, as David Stockman did initially, and reverses the relevant causal arrows, as monetarist supply-siders do when they insist that it is the money supply that causes inflation.

The muddle of supply-side praxis, however, is of secondary importance. The major threat of Reaganomics is to the very stability of the system. Its redistributive policies are not based on or derived from either supply-side school. Reaganomics is a counterrevolution in search of a legitimating theory and will use any convenient theory at hand to justify what is, at bottom, a raw power play that threatens to divide the nation along income lines and reduce it to a state of class conflict.

Notes

[1] Note that there was no suggestion to rescind or stretch out the cut in the top rate on *investment* income (from 70 to 50 percent) already in place as of January 1, 1982, or the June 10, 1981, cut in capital gains (from 28 to 20 percent) for those at the top of the income tax brackets. Those came early and all at once. The Senate Finance Committee on March 5, 1982, released new IRS estimates showing that 44 percent of all capital gains on the sale of securities, commodities, and other forms of wealth went unreported. The Trojan horse has obviously broken out into a gallop.

[2] *Wall Street Journal*, February 10, 1982.

[3] One hard-core, unrepentant classical supply-sider, Paul Craig Roberts, called the budget deficit a "red herring" in the *New York Times*, February 14, 1982. In his judgment, deficits were "to be measured in terms of the size of the economy and the saving pool available to finance them"—the latter, of course, to be abundantly stimulated by the supply-side tax cuts to the rich, thereby skirting the crowding-out problem. Besides, in his opinion, "budget deficits merely reflect the state of the economy" and with the economy in recession the deficit is not surprising. The question is, Why is the economy down? Roberts' answer is the Federal Reserve's erratic policies which have led to high interest rates. The deficit is therefore to be parked at the Federal Reserve's doorstep.

[4] As did the Reagan administration in its original ERP Report of February 1981. See pp. 89 and 90 above.

[5] There is, apparently, disagreement within the Federal Reserve itself, with the President of the powerful New York Bank, Anthony M. Solomon, arguing that financial innovations were complicating the problem of controlling the money

supply. See his talk before the Joint Luncheon of the American Economic and American Finance Associations, December 28, 1981, in Washington, D.C. (reprinted in the *1981 Annual Report* of the Federal Reserve Bank of New York). In an earlier speech in New York (March 26, 1981), he questioned that control of the money supply would, of itself, be enough to bring inflation under control and suggested that to depend on such control "does the economy a real disservice." In his view, the wage and price policies of labor and management *and budgetary deficits* tended to counteract successful monetary policy. "It would be a mistake," he said, "to assume that slowing monetary growth by itself offers a simple or painless, or purely technical solution to our inflation problem" (See *New York Times*, March 27, 1981, and *Challenge* magazine, March-April, 1982). The Federal Reserve, too, is obviously a troubled house.

[6]*New York Times*, January 28, 1982; italics supplied.

[7]Ibid.

CHAPTER 7

The Threat of Delegitimation

I

The viability of capitalism, in the past, has been based on its ability to accumulate capital without apparent limit and to realize a growth rate sufficient to allow an ever-increasing level of well-being broadly, though not necessarily equally, distributed across all strata of society. The long-term continuous growth that rapid accumulation made possible was based on the fusion of science and technology, and it was this dynamic aspect of capitalism that depoliticized the distribution of income. This certainly was the case from the latter half of the nineteenth century, starting with the triumph of the bourgeoisie in the consolidating revolutions of 1848, to World War I. It was during this remarkable period of almost half a century of relative peace that the revisionist Marxism of Eduard Bernstein softened the contours of revolutionary theory and led to the rise of social democratic parties on the continent of Europe, parties which have survived, in one form or another, to the present. A "just" society did not require a violent upheaval for its realization. The parliamentary system and the rise of trade unionism provided the better evolutionary route.

It was in this expansionary pre–World War I period that Max Weber formulated his views of society and the role of power in it.[1] Society was made up of unequals, of positively and negatively privileged classes. Power was in the hands of the highly privileged classes and it was they who had to establish a valid claim to legitimacy on legal, traditional, and charismatic grounds. For the ruling classes to be successful there had to be "a belief in the legality of enacted rules and the right of those elevated to authority under such rules to issue commands." And the legality of rules, and rulers, could not be in violation of long-standing traditions, nor could the ultimate leader be lacking in "the gift of grace." There had to be, in other words, a *myth* of the natural superiority of the ruling class acceptable to the negatively privileged classes of society. Domination, to be successful, had to effect a stable distribution of power. "Such a situation," wrote Weber, "exists as long as the masses continue in that natural state of theirs in which thought about the order of domination remains but little developed, which means, as long as no urgent needs render the state of affairs 'problematical.' "

The relative tranquillity of 1870 to 1914 was shattered in the First World War, in whose aftermath the unbending autocracy of Tsarist Russia was engulfed in the Bolshevik revolution. With this one exception of a country which had not been a part of the rapid development of capitalism in the West to begin with, the rapid growth of the industrialized nations resumed, though not without problems. Ten years later there was the Great Depression of the 1930s to be followed by World War II, and after World War II the great expansion of the postwar period from 1950 to the 1970s, to be followed by another spell of stagnation from 1974 to the present. The rhythm of capitalism had changed. Accumulation itself had become the "problematic," and with it the distribution of income and the very legitimacy of the system itself.

It was out of this concern for the nation's low growth rate that supply-side economics attempted to provide a scenario for the revitalization of capitalism. But unlike Keynesian demand-side policies, which place a greater reliance on the state, supply-side economics seeks to stimulate growth through a massive redistribution of income from the "negatively privileged" classes to the "highly privileged." In the past, capitalist accumulation had become the means by which the system was legitimized—a process of legitimation which, in effect, depoliticized the distribution of income by making it irrelevant as a social problem. Supply-side economics, however, is convinced that growth can be resumed only by a more unequal distribution of income in the short run—and thereafter one might add—in the expectation, to use Jack Kemp's JFK-metaphor, that a "rising tide lifts all boats," and that the tide will not come in without the prescribed change in the distribution of income. Supply-side economics seems to be engaged in a trade-off all its own—a trade-off of legitimacy for growth. It has broken the traditional linkage of the two since the inception of modern capitalism. And it is this breaking of the link that may well turn out to be an even bigger threat to the survival of the system than any bagful of Keynesian "interventions."

II

Reaganomics must be distinguished from supply-side theory, *per se*. The latter is not a coherent set of ideas, as we have seen. It is a flaky hodgepodge of half-digested ideas that can be roughly broken down into the classical and monetarist schools of supply-side economics—two schools which are fundamentally at odds. Overriding both are the budget-balancers in the President's Advisory Board, in the Office of Management and Budget, and in the House and Senate. Reaganomics picks and chooses from among the competing schools in order to justify its goal of redistributing wealth in favor of the wealthy. Its ultimate objective is redistribution whether or not it leads to economic growth. But if it can find a theory that says that its preferred redistribution of wealth and income will lead to greater growth, so much the better—if only for the sake of appearances.

The chances are that income, and the wealth from which it flows, will be more unevenly distributed *without* any accompanying stimulation of the growth of the economy. And if this, indeed, is the likely outcome, then in Weber's terms it is unlikely that "the masses [will] continue in that natural state of theirs in which thought about the order of domination remains but little developed." The social order could well become destabilized and delegitimated.

That the growth rate will be little affected by the redistribution policies of the Reagan administration is not difficult to explain. Reaganomics has accepted in full the classical supply-side argument for cutting taxes—especially on investment income. At the same time, the Laffer-curve effects of the tax cut have been dismissed by the President's own conservative and newly revised estimate of a cumulative budgetary deficit of $246 billion for the 1983-85 fiscal years—compared to the more realistic $389 billion cumulative deficit of the Congressional Budget Office. If we add to these cash budget deficits the off-budget items and the credit operations of the federal government, the total borrowings of the Treasury Department *for the 1983 fiscal year alone* could be well in excess of $200 billion. At the same time the administration supports the monetarist supply-side call for a fall in the growth rate of the money supply, against the wishes of the classical supply-side school. Whether it is sincere in this or not is beside the point. The Federal Reserve under Paul Volcker vows to keep a tight hand on the money supply in view of the appalling size of the federal deficits. Treasury borrowings, in short, will *not* be monetized. The head-on clash of the administration's fiscal and monetary policies will bring on the "crowding-out" effect as it has never been brought on before. Unless the bottom completely drops out, or the Federal Reserve has a change of heart, interest rates will soar, investment (capital accumulation) will fall, and so will output and employment. The net result will be high unemployment and a low growth rate—the classical supply-side tax cut notwithstanding. But although the much-touted increase in the growth rate will be nowhere in sight, the more unequal distribution of wealth and income will go on apace. And with rising unemployment and a worsening distribution of the social product, we will be moving rapidly toward a first-rate legitimation crisis.

In short, Reaganomics is not about growth. It is a raid on the public treasury in favor of the rich which, in its short-sightedness, may undermine the very interests of the highly privileged classes it seeks to promote. But then the Romanovs and the Bourbons were never known for their perspicacity. Neither was Marie Antoinette when she intoned "Qu'ils mangent de la brioche" as she unwittingly prepared for the blade.

III

Regardless of what happens to the rate of growth, the changes affecting the distribution of wealth and income will be more unequivocal, more lasting and more devastating in their long-run effects—and more difficult to reverse. The redistribution effects will be the result of two sets of related policies. One has to do with the planned cuts in personal income taxes, the cut in capital gains taxes as a result of the cut in the maximum rate on investment income from 70 to 50 percent, and the virtual abolishment of inheritance taxes, not to mention the specially tailored tax cuts and shelters for special-interest groups that so disturbed David Stockman. The other set of redistributive policies has to do with the expenditure side of the federal budget—cuts in nondefense expenditures and the "New Federalism" gambit for shifting federal expenditures onto state and local governments.

The well-to-do have been well taken care of by the tax cuts with some tax benefits accruing on a much smaller scale to the middle classes. The poor, of course, by virtue of being poor, have been virtually left out in the tax-cut cold. But they have not been forgotten on the expenditure side.

The cuts in nondefense expenditures have been largely concentrated on the poor and on some elements of the middle classes. The rich, if affected, have been more than compensated by their disproportionate share of the tax cuts. Paying the full cost of their children's education at an elite college or university should pose no great problem for them. Their increase in after-tax income should more than make up for the cuts in supplemental opportunity grants, direct student loans, educational Social Security payments, work-study programs, and Pell grants to needy students—to the limited extent that the well-to-do would have been affected by them to begin with.

On the other hand, the holes in the much-touted safety net for the poor are now big enough for most of the poor to slip through. There were an estimated 11.4 million families out of a total of 60.3 million in 1980 earning less than $10,000 a year. At least half will be affected by the spending cuts. In the administration's first round of cuts proposed in February 1981, the *net effect* of spending and tax cuts was positive for those earning $22,900 and above and negative for those below $22,900. The estimates in Table 7.1 were provided by a private business research and consulting firm (A. Gary Schilling and Company). The table speaks for itself.

Table 7.1 Fiscal Policy Effects by 1985
($ billion)

Household Income	Spending Cuts	Tax Cuts	Net Effect
-11,500	–$38.5	+$ 13.7	– $ 24.8
11,500-22,900	–$65.5	+$ 59.6	– $ 5.9
22,900-47,800	–$42.5	+$136.3	+$ 93.8
47,800 +	–$12.0	+$151.8	+$139.8

A more recent study by the Congressional Budget Office in February 1982 analyzed the effect of the administration's policies on the poorest families receiving annual incomes of $10,000 a year or less, and on the most affluent with incomes of $80,000 or more. The total population for fiscal 1983 will be approximately 225 million consisting of 60 million families and 27 million unrelated individuals. The poorest, with incomes of less than $10,000 a year, will make up approximately 14 million families; the most affluent, with incomes over $80,000 a year, account for about 600 thousand families. The CBO took into consideration the changes in Social Security, civil service and military pensions, unemployment insurance, food stamps, welfare, Medicaid, Medicare, guaranteed student loans, school lunches, housing assistance, veterans' benefits, and a few others. It also looked at the distribution of the tax cuts in fiscal 1983 by income class to compute the net effect of the expenditure and tax cuts on the various income classes. Twenty-three percent of all families will be in the poorest category in 1983—as compared with 18.9 percent in 1980. They will realize an average cut of $360 in benefits and a gain of $120 in taxes, leaving them with an average net *loss* of $240 per family. The most affluent families, making up 1 percent of the total number of families, will have an average cut of $120 in benefits but a windfall gain of $15,250 in tax cuts, netting them, on the average, $15,130. The poorest are the only income class to have a net loss. All others have a net gain with the gain increasing rapidly as one climbs the household income scale. All told, there will be an $82 billion tax cut in 1983 with a $17.5 billion cut in Federal benefit programs—assuming the President's February 1982 budget program goes through Congress unscathed, which it will not. Of the $17.5 billion cut in benefits, 40 percent will come from those receiving under $10,000 a year, and 67 percent from those families earning $20,000 or less. The benefit loss of families receiving $40,000 a year or more will be 11 percent, but then they will get one-half the projected $82 billion cut in personal income taxes.

The New York State Office of Federal Affairs computed the federal reductions in state grants from 1981 to 1983 in nominal and real terms. Table 7.2 lists those program cuts that would most affect the poor, in millions of dollars. The reductions in real terms are based on the CBO's estimate of a 14.4 percent inflation rate over the two-year span 1981 to 1983.

It is clear that the nation is moving from President Johnson's "War on Poverty" to President Reagan's "War on the Poor." Of the 6 million families below the government's official poverty line, approximately 3.6 million are whites and 1.7 million are blacks. But the 1.7 million blacks are about 30 percent of all black families compared to 7 percent for the 3.6 million whites. The poor, in other words, are disproportionately black. The poor, black or white, are generally not part of the productive labor force. They are poorly educated and poorly organized. They are the disenfranchised lacking in economic or political weight. Not surprisingly

Table 7.2 **Federal Grant Reductions**
($ millions)

	1981 Appropriations	1983 Proposals	Percent Reductions 1981-83	Percent Reductions Adjusted For Inflation
Community-service block grants	$ 472	$ 100	79%	97%
CETA employment and training	7,100	2,000	70	84
Vocational and adult education	786	500	36	50
Social service block grants	2,900	1,900	34	48
Low-income energy assistance	1,905	1,300	31	45
Child-welfare block grant	522	380	27	42
Child nutrition	3,600	3,200	11	25

Source: New York State Office of Federal Affairs, February 1982.

they are being made to bear the greater burden of the cuts in social expenditures, at a time when defense expenditures are rapidly mounting and taxes are being cut, especially for the well-off. And since the cuts in taxes exceed the cuts in total expenditures, deficits are looming large—generating calls for further cuts in social expenditures. But the poor are being told that, in time, the supply-side policies of the administration will so stimulate economic growth that they will be pulled out of their poverty by a tidal wave of activity. In the meantime, and until the supply-side policies have their intended effect, what is to be done to alleviate the increased short-run suffering of the poor? Charity!

President Reagan is calling for a "spirit of shared sacrifice" to provide private substitutes for the reduced government welfare programs. Philanthropy is to be rekindled. But, said the President in his address to New York Partnership, Inc., at the Waldorf Astoria on January 14, 1982, "I don't want to leave the impression that our administration is asking the private sector to fill the gap, dollar for dollar, for every reduction in the federal budget. We don't want you to duplicate wasteful and unnecessary programs." There was no danger that *he* would be doing so. In 1980 out of a gross income of $227,968, the President had given $3,085 to charity. President Nixon tried to give $576,000 to himself in charitable contributions by contributing his Vice-Presidential papers to the National Archives, but the deduction was disallowed. He did give, however, a total of $13,481 to charities from 1969 to 1972 (ranging from $295 in 1972 to $7,512 in 1970) out of an adjusted gross income of $1,122,364—most of this modest amount going to such organizations for the poor as the Billy Graham Evangelical Association, The Eisenhower Medical Center, the American Red Cross, and the Boys Club of America. President Ford's $5,984 in charitable contributions out of an adjusted gross income of $147,683 in 1974 went to similar organizations. Born-again President Carter did better. From 1976 to 1979 he gave $72,625 out of $653,470—from his book royalties on *Why Not the Best*—but it went to a religious foundation and the Plains Baptist Church.[2]

Earlier, the Executive Director of the Stanley M. Isaacs Neighborhood Foundation in New York had appealed to eighty-five large food manufacturers for food donations to be used for distribution to homebound elderly people. She received nothing. "The response of the corporate community," she wrote, "was especially dismaying since President Reagan seems so assured that it will compensate for decreased public funding." Corporations, she observed, "are significant supporters of not-for-profit endeavors when their gifts carry significant tax write-offs or corporate visibility. When the gift does not have these advantages, corporations tend to stay away."[3] Leaders of private charities quickly expressed dismay over the President's approach. Still the President persevered and said he was "counting on voluntary strength as we turn from government doing for us that which we can best do for ourselves." But if we can't, there is always, of course, the supply-side boost to the economy which will greatly diminish the need for charity.

IV

By February 1982, exactly one year after the original supply-side Economic Recovery Program had proclaimed the realization of balanced budgets from 1984 on, the administration's program was in shambles. The vaunted upsurge of the economy and the revenue effects of the celebrated Laffer curve were nowhere in sight. As far as the eye could see there were budget deficits well over the $100 billion-a-year mark. Despite his campaign promise to balance the budget, the President quickly shifted ground. Deficits weren't so bad after all, and the big guns of the classical supply-side school were marched to the front to proclaim the new line. Apart from the economic irrelevance of budget deficits, the argument now was that they would not have materialized had not the administration been "surprised" by the severe downturn of the economy in the latter half of 1981. That the downturn was itself due to the economic policies of the administration was not something which could be allowed—let alone recognized. Recessions were exogenous phenomena, like floods, earthquakes, and other natural disasters. Either that or they were the consequence of profligate Democratic administrations in the past. It would just take a little longer for the administration's economic policies to undo past stupidities and take full effect. In the meantime the 1982 congressional elections were drawing closer and many Republican congressmen were concerned that their political life was on the line. Recessions have never worked in favor of the party in power. The budget-balancers were making unwelcomed noises and finding allies among the formerly faithful in the Congress. There were calls for stretching out the tax cuts of 1981 and for increasing excise taxes. Worse still, the Defense Department budget was under moderate attack. Defense expenditures would have to be trimmed.

It was clearly necessary for the administration to do something to get the public's mind off the deficits. Early on in the administration, when the Secretary of State, Alexander Haig, took center stage and started beating the cold war drums over the issue of El

Salvador, it was felt that Haig was diverting attention from the President's economic program. The Secretary of State was told in no uncertain terms to keep the issue on the back burner. He dutifully complied. But with the economic program in serious trouble a year later, the Secretary of State was unleashed and El Salvador leaped once again into the headlines. Still, the deficits were not completely "crowded out" of the news—especially after David Stockman's revelations in *The Atlantic*. By January 1982 the Caribbean cauldron was put on one of the front burners and was joined on the other by a new diversionary tactic—the "New Federalism."

Even before the February 1982 budget was announced, calling for a second round of nondefense expenditure cuts, the states were already in trouble because of the original 1981 program of the administration. The states were not able to absorb those spending cuts which had been imposed, particularly in the various grants-in-aid programs that turn federal tax dollars over to state and local governments. At the end of fiscal 1980, according to the National Governor's Association, the year-end balance of state governments, as a percentage of the year's expenditures from their general operating funds, was 9 percent.[4] By the end of fiscal 1981 it had dropped to 3.3 percent and was due to fall to 1.5 percent by the end of fiscal 1982, all this before enactment of the 1981 federal budget and tax cuts. Now the states were faced with a 25 percent reduction in federal support for social services. On top of the expenditure cuts, the federal tax cut itself would cause a drop in state tax revenues since most states had tied their corporate and personal tax rates to the federal rates and depreciation schedules. The states were faced with falling revenues along with falling federal aid. They would either have to raise their own taxes directly, or decouple from the federal rates, in order to maintain social services, or alternatively, to avoid the wrath of their electorate, leave tax rates where they are while pruning severely their level of social services for the disenfranchised. The chances were that they would have to both raise taxes *and* cut down on social expenditures. In effect, the federal administration was trying to put its own budget house in order by setting fire to those of the states. But then, of course, the states could appeal for private philanthropic charity from the rich who had fared so well under the supply-side policies of the federal administration.

When it became clear early in 1982 that the federal government's budget would hardly be in balance by 1984, despite its earlier attempt to foist a significant part of its deficits onto the states, the screw was turned another notch. The details of the "New Federalism" were announced in the President's January 26, 1982, State of the Union Message to Congress. The states were to take over forty federal grant programs covering education, highways, subways, sewers, and such social services as food stamps, aid to families with dependent children, and other welfare expenditures. In turn the federal government would assume all responsibility for Medicaid. The goal of the New Federalism was to "take the country back to the Constitution" by reestablishing states' rights and responsibilities. If state legislatures chose to do away with certain types of social expenditures—originally undertaken at the prodding of the federal government—they would be free to do so. The New Federalism was to be a "new partnership." To ease the pain of transition the federal government would establish, through 1987, a $28 billion-a-year Federal Trust Fund financed out of existing excise taxes on cigarettes, alcohol, tobacco, and gasoline. After 1987 the Trust Fund would be gradually reduced to $7 billion a year and disappear by 1991. In nine years the states would be on their own, and so would the underprivileged.

For the 1984 fiscal year alone, the "turnback programs" would cost the states $30.2 billion plus $16.5 billion for the absorption of AFDC and food stamps, or a total of $46.7 billion. In return the states would receive, in the aggregate, $28 billion from the Trust Fund and be relieved of $19.1 billion of Medicaid expenses which the federal government would take over—or a total of $47.1 billion in savings and temporary aid. On the face of it, it would be an equal swap, so long as the Trust Fund existed. After 1987, the states would either have to raise their taxes or cut back on their social services, or both. The "Great Swap and Turnback" program, in support of the Constitution as President Reagan saw it, had been launched.

The Democratic Speaker of the House, Tip O'Neill, called it "a disguised [sic] attempt to balance the budget on the backs of state and local governments"—and on the backs of the disenfranchised poor, he could have added. The Republican governor of Vermont, Richard A. Snelling, called it "an economic Bay of Pigs," with the conservative Republican mayor of Cleveland, George V. Voinovich, referring to it as "a meat axe." And the Democratic-Republican mayor of New York, Ed Koch, who had earlier flirted with the Reagan administration, dismissed the New Federalism as "a sham and a shame."

State and local governments were faced with tax revolts even before President Reagan came to power, and the Reagan recession had already cut deeply into their revenues over and above what the administration had already taken away. They were in the process of raising regressive excise taxes to meet their budget deficits and were reluctant to raise them further. According to a Joint Economic Committee study of the forty-eight largest cities, twenty had increased their taxes in 1981, thirty-one had increased their fees and user taxes, and eighteen had deferred needed capital projects. Hugh Carey, the governor of New York, called the New Federalism the "New Feudalism," and governors across the country were up in arms. Patrick Moynihan, the neo-conservative senator from New York, predicted that the New Federalism would force state governments, on the average, to raise taxes by 8.81 percent in fiscal 1984, or by $13.2 billion—either that or cut their social programs by nearly one-third. Given that state taxes, especially those levied on income, have as much of a supply-side incentive effect as federal taxes, the New Federalism was in danger of sabotaging its own program for economic growth—assuming the arguments of supply-side theory to be correct.

By March 1982 it didn't seem that the New Federalism was going anywhere. By the end of April it was dead. Attention was refocused on the administration's projected deficits of $246 billion from 1983 through 1985, and the Congressional Budget Office's $389 billion estimate for the same time period. Other projections ran higher still. On April 30, the Reagan administration agreed to use $182 billion as the projected deficit for fiscal year 1983 alone, assuming no new tax and expenditure cuts in 1983. It was to form the basis for budget negotiations with the Congress. The idea of a balanced budget in the foreseeable future had been shot down by the administration itself. Wall Street takes news like this badly and Paul Volcker will no doubt pledge the Federal Reserve to a renewed effort of monetary restraint. An enormous "crowding-out" effect will either keep interest rates up or push them even higher with the prospect of a prolonged recession and rising unemployment. For the first time since the Great Depression of the 1930s talk of a major economic collapse was in the open.[5] The international community responded. The American economy was too big to be ignored. The economic policies of the Reagan administration had become a threat to the entire Western alliance.

V

As early as September 1979, Japan and West Germany began raising their interest rates to fight inflation, causing the U.S. dollar to drop sharply on the foreign exchange markets. The then Chairman of the House Banking Committee, Congressman Henry Reuss, objected to the mounting pressure to raise U.S. interest rates and argued that "Germany, Japan and other situated [countries] should fight their domestic inflation in a way that will not endanger the world's currency, the dollar, or induce the United States to risk turning a recession into a depression that could sink the whole free world." The German Finance Minister, Hans Matthoefer, was unmoved by the congressman's concerns. Germany was not about to accept higher inflation because of American criticism. "We won't make inflation [here]," he said, "because of our American friends." That was in September. In October Paul Volcker came on the scene. The Federal Reserve would henceforth follow a monetarist policy and target the monetary base with interest rates free to go where they will in response to market forces. And indeed they did. They soared. Capital flowed into American financial markets and the U.S. dollar climbed, and climbed, and climbed. The American economy is a giant compared to that of Germany or Japan. The shoe was now on the other foot. And memories are mercifully short.

By February 1981 the West German Chancellor, Helmut Schmidt, was expressing concern over the new U.S. President's economic program. High U.S. interest rates threatened to deepen the European recession. The Chancellor was a budget-balancer. He advised the United States to match its proposed supply-side tax cut with cuts in government expenditures in order to relieve the pressure on U.S. interest rates. The "crowding-out" effect was as much a part of German thinking as it was of the monetarists ensconced in the U.S. Treasury. High U.S. interest rates were "destructive" to the world economy and, in Helmut Schmidt's opinion, "absolutely unacceptable." By June 1981, Italy and France had joined the chorus. The Italian Foreign Minister, Emilio Colombo, met with the new French Socialist Foreign Minister, Claude Cheysson, in Rome. After their three-hour conference, Mr. Colombo said, "We are the trusted allies of the United States, but we ask them to understand the serious consequences that [their monetary] policy has for us." Back in Paris, the French Foreign Minister lashed out. "With interest rates at 20 percent and the dollar floating in the stratosphere, employment is falling, trade suffers, no industrial investments can take place and the worse-off are in the forefront of the battle against inflation." Reaganomics, in other words, threatened to sabotage the new socialist government's priority of reducing unemployment. Now it was the turn of the United States to reject the criticism of the Europeans. Meyer Rashish, the U.S. Under Secretary of State for Economic Affairs, struck back. U.S. economic policy was designed to restore economic growth without inflation. "We are not pursuing a policy of high interest rates," he said. Still, with the value of the dollar mounting and with oil denominated in U.S. dollars, the European economic recovery was being stunted.

With a consistency to be admired, Congressman Reuss, now Chairman of the Joint Economic Committee, sided with the Europeans, calling for an economic policy to fight inflation in the United States and an easing of monetary restraint to bring interest rates down. The congressman is obviously not a monetarist, nor is he a supply-sider. Jacques de Larosière, the head of the International Monetary Fund, spoke out in July and warned against an excessive reliance on monetary policy to fight inflation. Next to speak out was Gaston Thorn, the President of the European Commission. The high U.S. interest rates were draining investment capital from Europe and U.S. economic policy had become insensitive to the problems of Europe. "Voices in our wide political spectrum," he warned, "are saying more and more loudly: 'You're unemployed because of the Americans: You have no job because the United States is strengthening its economy so it can be richer and stronger—at your expense.'"

By mid-July the U.S. Secretary of the Treasury, Donald T. Regan, assured the Europeans that the surge in U.S. interest rates was temporary. After all, the level of interest rates was simply a matter of demand and supply, he argued, and a tight monetary policy was the only way to bring down the rate of inflation. The Europeans should be patient. The supply-side fiscal policy of the U.S. administration would soon lead to an expansion of the U.S. economy and bring the U.S. budget back into balance. The "crowding-out" effect would disappear as a result, and interest rates would come tumbling down. With the U.S. economy on the move again, with low inflation and low interest rates, the European economies would bask in the wise policies of the U.S. administration. Trust the U.S. It knows what it is doing.

François Mitterand, the new socialist President of France, was not impressed. France could not wait. U.S. interest rates had to be brought down now. A new German Minister of Economics, Otto Graff Lambsdorff, scoffed at the supply-side nostrums of the Reagan administration. "I am doubtful," he said, "that the tax cut will mean revitalizing capital expenditures, and I ask Secretary

Regan where he got the evidence that it would generate saving and investment and not consumption." The answer, of course, is Jack Kemp, Arthur Laffer, Jude Wanniski, and George Gilder—the four economics "experts" of the Reagan administration—not to mention the two undersecretaries of the U.S. Treasury, Norman Ture and Beryl Sprinkel. At any rate, in Mr. Lambsdorff's opinion, the Reagan administration was overloading monetary policy and driving up interest rates as a result.

Despite the chorus of protest from across the Atlantic, the ten members of the European Economic Community were hopelessly divided. Great Britain under Margaret Thatcher ruthlessly pursued her own version of supply-side economics and monetarism. The summer of 1981 had seen riots in the streets and the Labour Party had been split in two. Germany, for the first time, was experiencing a recession with high levels of unemployment and was still following conservative neoclassical economic policies, while France, under the socialist leadership of François Mitterand, had reverted to Keynesian policies to fight its stagnation and unemployment. The overall economic situation in Europe was dismal and fears were expressed that a trade war with the United States would lead to protectionist policies and the inward spiraling of international trade. Parallels to the 1930s were not hard to find.

By February 1982, the European countries lashed out at the economic policies of the Reagan administration. The storm had been brewing for over a year. The news of the huge U.S. deficits in February were intolerable to the Europeans. Finance Minister Jacques Delors of France, Chancellor of the Exchequer Sir Geoffrey Howe of Britain, Finance Minister Willie de Clercq of Belgium, and Karl Otto Pöhl, president of the West German central bank, viewed the new deficit projections as a threat to the world's economic health.[6] The size of the deficits, in their view, would certainly raise interest rates and unemployment in Europe, with the U.S. dollar rising even higher. With European unemployment at 10 percent, this was an intolerable state of affairs. Indeed, at 16 million European unemployment was the highest since the Great

Depression. The French warned that the U.S. deficits could "push the world into a depression." "I cannot believe," said the head of the German central bank, "that the United States does not understand that it bears responsibility not only for its own economy, but also for the world." The Western alliance was being undermined, and fears were raised about a rupture in monetary cooperation with the United States.

It was Chancellor Schmidt, however, who raised the gravest issue of all. "What I fear," he said, "is economic and social destabilization." Europe well remembers the 1930s and the political consequences of the Great Depression. A massive crisis was in the making not only domestically in the United States but internationally as well.

And what advice did the European leaders give the President? The United States should raise taxes and cut its expenditures further in order to bring the deficits under control! The bankruptcy of economic policy is apparently not restricted to American shores.

And what was President Reagan's response to this European storm of protest? "We think . . . that the outlook for the Western economy is good. We will get over the short-term problems." In the meantime, he would prefer that we turn our attention to the threat of Communism and the danger of Russian expansionism.

VI

That is where things stand at this writing in the spring of 1982. What of the future? There is a contingency in history that precludes all prediction. We do indeed live in a world of uncertainty. Still, history is not capriciously arbitrary. It is not pure happenstance. We are, it seems, headed for a legitimation crisis over the distribution of the social product both domestically and internationally.

The economic policies of the Reagan administration are barely one year old. They have already gone through one major modification concerning the acceptability of deficits. For the moment the

President is holding his supply-side ground. His tax cuts are not to be altered, he opposes "revenue enhancement" via excise tax increases, and he continues to support the "monetary rule" of the monetarists—despite the defection, on this issue, of his classical supply-side supporters. Originally, the President sought to increase the rate of growth, solve the problem of inflation, and balance the budget. The latter was to be achieved through the Laffer-effect of his tax cut. The tax cut was to lead to an offsetting increase in the government's tax revenues, or at least one sufficient, with the cuts in government expenditures, to reduce the budget deficits significantly and more or less resolve the "crowding-out" problem, which is itself the direct consequence of his restrictive monetary policy and the failure to bring the federal deficits under control. Nonmonetization of the public debt is an absolute article of faith. The administration has become enmeshed in its own contradiction of an expansionary fiscal policy to promote growth (through tax cuts only partially offset by cuts in government expenditures) and a restrictive monetary policy to control inflation.

There are several reasons why the tax cuts were only partially offset by the cuts of government expenditures. One has to do with the "surprise" of the 1981-82 deep recession and the consequent increase in the unemployment rate. The rise in unemployment by roughly two percentage points in the latter half of 1981 automatically added $60 billion to the deficit. But apart from the failure of supply-side fiscal policy to stimulate output and government tax revenues, the cut in social expenditures has been offset, by and large, by the increase in defense expenditures. Over the next six years, the President's February 1982 plan is to spend $1.6 trillion, or an average of $267 billion a year, on the military. For the fiscal years 1982 and 1983, defense outlays will increase by $33.1 billion or by 18.1 percent in nominal terms and 10.5 percent in real terms (adjusted for inflation). The increase in obligational authority is bigger still, as Table 7.3 indicates.

The fiscal 1984 budgetary outlay for military purposes is scheduled for $247 billion, or an increase of 14.4 percent. Overall, from

1982 to 1987, whereas the President had originally called for a 7 percent annual increase in military budget authority *in real terms*, the figure is now programmed to increase at an annual real rate of 7.5 percent. On those terms the military budget *in 1982 dollars* will be $307.5 billion by 1987 or $400 billion in current prices, almost double the 1982 figure.

With the three-year supply-side tax cut of 1981, the sharp downturn in output and employment in the latter part of 1981, and the whopping increases in defense expenditures, it is not at all surprising that the Reagan administration has generated enormous deficits for each of the next five years. One does not normally expect to balance the budget by cutting taxes and in-

Table 7.3. Fiscal Year Defense Expenditures ($ billion)

	1982	1983	Increase	Percent Increase Nominal	Real
Outlays	$182.8	$215.9	$33.1	18.4%	10.5%
Obligational Authority	$214.2	$258.0	$43.8	20.4%	13.3%

creasing, or failing to reduce, the level of government expenditures—not if one can add and subtract properly. Not surprisingly the power is shifting away from the supply-siders (who now like good Keynesians play down the significance of deficits) to the budget-balancers and their ideological allies in the House and Senate. The President's 1983 budget, which initially projected a conservative $92 billion deficit by making conveniently optimistic assumptions concerning the growth rate, the rate of inflation, and the level of interest rates, will not get through Congress unchanged. The faithful of 1981 are in revolt. The Republican Chairman of the Senate Budget Committee, Pete V. Domenici, wants to decrease the real rate of growth in defense expenditures to 5 percent through 1985, disallow the cost-of-living increases in entitlement programs, including Social Security, and increase taxes by $122 over the next three years. The Senate majority leader, Howard Baker, has proposed a federal income surtax, while the House minority leader, Robert H. Michel, advocated deferral of the 1982 ten percent tax cut and the repeal of the tax indexing proposal scheduled to take effect in 1985. Still others may try to paint the President into a corner by refusing to raise the national debt limit, thereby forcing him to increase taxes, cut the defense budget, and freeze outlays on Medicaid, Medicare, and veterans' retirement benefits. Other proposals are to repeal the corporate selling of tax credits (which alone will cost the government $26 billion in revenue over a four-year period), stretch out the three-year tax cut on personal income, and impose a federal sales tax.

The Congress is required by the Budget Act to adopt a first budget resolution by May 15, although it may postpone any action until after the November 1982 congressional elections. Whatever happens, it is clear that the administration has lost control of its own economic policies. The early 1981 days of euphoria are apparently gone forever. Rather than a grand design, no matter how ill-conceived, economic policy now lacks any coherence, ideological or otherwise, as the special-interest groups seek to protect their flanks and congressmen form regional alliances among themselves in order to come out of the bedlam with a few politically marketable marbles for their constituents.

After one year, the supply-side house is ready to collapse around the heads of the benighted supply-siders within who are too busy arguing among themselves to question the validity of their beliefs. In the end, the budget-balancers may well win the day, although budget balancing is hardly a theory upon which to base a set of economic policies. If they do gain the upper hand, further cuts in social expenditures can be expected—ones which will now hit the middle as well as the lower classes. As for the Pentagon budget, it is unlikely to be cut. All one can reasonably expect is a slowing down of its *real* rate of growth.

Early in March 1982, at the urging of the Senate majority leader,

Howard Baker, the business community responded to the President's latest projections of budgetary deficits. The prestigious Business Roundtable, made up of the chief executives of 200 major corporations, made its views known. The President's deficits were unacceptable. Led by Clifton C. Garvin, Chairman of the Exxon Corporation, the Roundtable Policy Committee called for a slowing down of the real growth rate of military expenditures, a deferral of the 10 percent 1983 tax cut, and further cuts in the indexed nondefense entitlement expenditures of the federal government. What drew their fire, in particular, was the high level of interest rates. "We are deeply concerned," said the 46-member Policy Committee, "by continuing high interest rates . . . . *We believe that interest rates and the projected deficits are interrelated* and that without a sharp drop in interest rates no reasonable recovery will be seen before the fourth quarter." They were joined in their concern by the U.S. Chamber of Commerce, the National Association of Manufacturers, and the American Business Conference.[7] Since deficits cause high interest rates, the only way to lower them (according to the Roundtable) is to lower the deficits—thus avoiding the "crowding-out" effect of the Federal Reserve's tight money policy. And the principal way to lower the deficits, as the elite of the business community see it, is to raise taxes and lower social expenditures—*in a time of severe unemployment!* Not a word about easing up on the money supply in order to bring down interest rates. We have, apparently, learned nothing from the days of Herbert Hoover. The business establishment has clearly joined forces with the financial community and the budget-balancers against the supply-siders. The President continues to resist all efforts to adjust his policies. The struggle is on and if the budget-balancers have their way, as seems likely, Reaganomics will have gone under. But whether the budget-balancers or the supply-siders win is of minor importance. In either event, the economy will worsen in the absence of some unforeseen exogenous jolt.

And no matter who ultimately gets control, no matter what coalition succeeds in applying ad hoc "solutions" to the large budgetary deficits, the fact remains that the distribution of wealth and income will have been changed structurally, with the underclass coming out the worse for it. A Catholic bishop testifying before the House Budget Committee in early 1982 reminded the committee members of a speech by Pope John Paul II a year earlier, in which he said: "The present economic difficulties . . . must not become a pretext for giving in to the temptation to make the poor pay for the solutions to the problems of the rich." Bishop Sullivan of Brooklyn was obviously not privy to the mysteries of supply-side economics. Solving the problems of the rich automatically solves the problems of the poor. It is only when we misguidedly try to exact, involuntarily, charity from the rich, by forcing them to pay higher taxes, that the poor suffer the most.

To cut taxes without affecting the distribution of income and to impose an incomes policy to control inflation while bringing down interest rates by easing up on the money supply would be to slip, unpardonably, into Post Keynesian heresy. Although the good bishop could not have had the theories of Max Weber in mind, they are much to the point. With the return of the economic royalists and the collapse of Reaganomics, the budget-balancers will, like Herbert Hoover in his day, raise taxes and cut nondefense expenditures in order at least to reduce the deficit if an outright balance is not immediately attainable. And as in Hoover's time, the bottom could drop out. Social turmoil and unrest would follow in that event. As Chancellor Schmidt put it before the fact, "The fabric of the economy and society is endangered by the deepest recession since the middle 30s"—although he, too, is calling for the United States to raise its taxes and cut its expenditures to bring the budget in balance!

When a society is seen no longer to care about the welfare of the majority of its people, when it is perceived to be in the hands of a greedy and profligate minority, the legitimacy of the system is cast in doubt. And from this anything can follow. I personally doubt that revolutionary violence will break out. I doubt that the country will move to the Left. As the lower middle class sees its position eroded, the chances are that it will regard the unemployed lower classes a threat to its own well-being and turn against them in a class warfare based on race. In response to a legitimation crisis, the political response could as well be to the Right. It has happened before, but there are no inevitabilities in history. Another possibility is for a pragmatic groping for solutions that would restore the legitimacy of the system, as indeed was done by the New Deal in the 1930s. But such an approach is precisely what the Reagan administration, in its own benighted way, has rejected out of hand. We may well end up turning full circle, but at an unnecessary cost in human suffering. Blind ideology and people who propound favored economic theories with religious fervor are not known for their sense of doubt, or for nuance, or for their sensitivity to the needs and feelings of others. Nor are they to be trusted with power. God save us from those who know where paradise is and who insist on taking us there even if they have to drag us kicking and screaming all the way. And may God protect us from those who, for their own ulterior purposes, cynically use those who claim to know as their stalking horses.

VII

Western capitalism is once again faced with a major crisis. With economic growth sagging, the distribution of the social product has been repoliticized. In the past, Western capitalism exhibited an almost infinite if somewhat imperfect capacity to adapt to external shocks and changed circumstances. Its response to the the economic crisis of the 1970s, however, has been along two different paths. In Japan and Germany the government looms large, particularly in Japan where it has taken a direct hand in raising the level of private investment in the economy. The 1981 socialist victory of François Mitterand in France followed by that of Andreas Papandreou in Greece presages a movement toward a *planned* form of capitalism, their "socialist" trappings notwithstanding. The goal is to relegitimate the system, after years of right-wing policies, through Post Keynesian policies aimed at a more equitable distribution of income and the reattainment of full employment—

particularly of their youth.

In England and the United States, on the other hand, an opposite tack is being taken. The welfare state is being dismantled and the economy deregulated. Both Margaret Thatcher and Ronald Reagan are following supply-side policies wedded to a doctrinaire monetarism whose ultimate result will be to increase the inequality of income without increasing the rate of economic growth. Margaret Thatcher's England poses no real threat to continental Europe, but the United States is too massive an economy not to have a profound effect on the economies of all other nations. At the same time, supply-side economics in the United States is being coupled with a bellicose foreign policy that requires massive increases in arms expenditures, thus giving the arms race another fateful twist upward. Arms expenditures, it should be noted, add nothing to the productive capacity of the economy. The average productivity of a nuclear bomb is zero. But arms expenditures have a "crowding-out" effect all their own and serve not only to distort the allocation of resources but to brake the potential long-term growth rate. It is not by accident that those economies which spend more on arms have had, in the postwar period, the lowest growth rates and the highest levels of unemployment.

Should supply-side economics fail in the United States, as I expect it to do, it might well be followed by a search for scapegoats and an even more violent lurch to the Right. In that event, Western capitalism will have lost its vaunted ability to adapt. The Western alliance could crumble in a renewed cold war between the two major superpowers of the world with widespread dissension among the former allies. The stakes are high, the future murky. We may yet stumble out of it by returning to our senses and going forward, not backward.

The fact remains that Reaganomics is a redistribution gambit based on a crude resurgence of nineteenth-century social Darwinism. It cynically seeks its theoretical justification in supply-side economics—itself a jumble of confusion, as befits the product of mediocre, midget minds. Reaganomics is no more scientific than faith healing is. Only in the case of Reaganomics it is the "laying off" of hands that will, supposedly, lead to our redemption. Government is to withdraw. It has no positive role to play in seeking solutions to critical social problems. And it has no responsibility to its people other than to leave them to their own devices. That government is best which governs least and thus releases the creative powers of "the people." But who are "the people"? At what ideal and meaningless level of abstraction are we operating? The problem of any complex society is power, and power is the final arbiter of the distribution of the social product among "the people." The rise of government in democratic societies, historically, has been in response to the excesses of private economic power. And it has been the intermediation of government that has, however imperfectly, legitimated the system and kept it in a precarious balance. And it is this precarious balance that Reaganomics now threatens to undo in the name of a rampant form of capitalism. The economic royalists have returned, and like most royalists they have learned nothing from the past. *Ah! ça ira, ça ira, ça ira* . . .

Notes

[1] *Economy and Society,* 2 vols., University of California Press, 1978. All quotations are taken from this edition of his work, Chapter 3, p. 215, and Chapter 10, pp. 953-54.

[2] *New York Times,* January 22, 1982.

[3] Carol Tweedy, Letter to the Editor, *New York Times,* November 14, 1981.

[4] *New York Times,* October 11, 1981.

[5] See Kenneth H. Bacon, "Still a Minority View, Depression Fear Grows," front-page column in the *Wall Street Journal,* February 22, 1982, and Benjamin J. Stein, "A Scenario for a Depression," Sunday Magazine Section, *New York Times,* February 28, 1982.

[6] *New York Times,* February 13 and 18, 1982.

[7] *New York Times,* March 4, 1982.

About the Author

Stephen Rousseas is Dexter M. Ferry, Jr., Professor of Economics at Vassar. Previously he taught at Columbia, the University of Michigan, Yale, Cornell, and New York University. Professor Rousseas is the author of *The Death of Democracy: Greece and the American Conscience* (1967), *Monetary Theory* (1972), *Capitalism and Catastrophe: A Critical Appraisal of the Limits to Capitalism* (1979), and numerous articles and reviews.

DATE DUE

NOV 23 1983	NOV 0 9 2009
DEC 07 1983	
DEC 14 1983	
APR 25 1984	
AUG 28 1985	
APR 29 1987	
FEB 24 1988	
MAR 28 1988	
APR 20 1988	
DEC 22 1994	
NOV 24 1997	
DEC 22 1997	
MAY 06 1998	
DEC 14 1998	
APR 28 1999	

DEMCO 38-297